W9-BZK-793

LEARN
Spanish
in a Hurry

GRASP
THE BASICS OF
español
PRONTO!

Julie Gutin

Adams Media
Avon, Massachusetts

Copyright ©2006, F+W Publications, Inc.
All rights reserved. This book, or parts thereof, may not be reproduced
in any form without permission from the publisher; exceptions are
made for brief excerpts used in published reviews.

Published by
Adams Media, an F+W Publications Company
57 Littlefield Street, Avon, MA 02322. U.S.A.
www.adamsmedia.com

ISBN 10: 1-59869-086-8
ISBN 13: 978-1-59869-086-6

Printed in the United States of America.

J I H G F E D C B A

Library of Congress Cataloging-in-Publication Data
available from the publisher

This publication is designed to provide accurate and authoritative
information with regard to the subject matter covered. It is sold with
the understanding that the publisher is not engaged in rendering legal,
accounting, or other professional advice. If legal advice or other expert
assistance is required, the services of a competent professional person
should be sought.

> —From a *Declaration of Principles* jointly adopted by a
> Committee of the American Bar Association and a
> Committee of Publishers and Associations

Many of the designations used by manufacturers and sellers to distinguish their product are claimed as trademarks. Where those designations
appear in this book and Adams Media was aware of a trademark claim,
the designations have been printed with initial capital letters.

Contains portions of material adapted and abridged from *The Everything®
Spanish Grammar Book* by Julie Gutin, ©2005, F+W Publications, Inc.;
The Everything® Spanish Verb Book by Laura K. Lawless, ©2004, F+W
Publications, Inc.; and *The Everything® Spanish Phrase Book* by Cari
Luna, ©2004, F+W Publications, Inc.

This book is available at quantity discounts for bulk purchases.
For information, please call 1-800-289-0963.

Contents

Introduction

So YOU'D LIKE to learn Spanish, and you need to do it fast. Maybe you've already booked a trip to sunny Dominican Republic or can't wait to explore the ancient Mayan cities of Peru. Maybe you just got a gig teaching English in Costa Rica or learning how to dance flamenco in Spain. Or maybe you just got a new job and knowing some Spanish would be a big help. Whatever your needs are, you are in a hurry. But can you really learn Spanish this quickly?

The good news is that, yes, you can. But it's going to take some effort. This book will help you take that first and crucial step—it'll give you all the basics you need to figure out the key concepts of Spanish grammar and get you started with building up your Spanish vocabulary. Use it as you would a map, to get you oriented and headed in the right direction, and you'll be on your way to mastering the Spanish language.

Remember—you can't get lazy! To learn Spanish, you'll need lots of practice. Fortunately, the opportunities are everywhere. Turn on the television—you may have a Spanish-speaking channel or two to choose from. Start with a soccer game, then move on to national news, and one day you'll be comfortable enough to watch a telenovela about a beautiful young woman and her tragic destiny. For lunch, skip the burger joint and head to a taco shop—you can order your burrito con pollo and chat up the server in Spanish. Pick up the local Spanish-language newspaper and start with the headlines. Then see if you can find an international pen pal to practice your Spanish writing. The opportunities for practice are endless!

The most important thing to remember is, keep it going! Language acquisition takes some effort, but it's well worth it. So keep reading, and you'll be speaking Spanish in no time!

01 / Beginning Spanish

WHERE DO YOU start when you want to learn Spanish in a hurry? The alphabet, of course! You cannot start forming words without understanding the building blocks! When children are beginning to speak English, one of the first things they learn is the Alphabet Song to learn about letters, and Spanish is no different.

Learn Your ABCs

If you remember the English alphabet, learning the Spanish version will be a snap: Because the Spanish alphabet is almost identical, all you have to do is memorize the pronunciation of each letter.

Pronunciation

The basics of Spanish pronunciation aren't difficult to master—only a few sounds don't have an equivalent in English. And learning to read is much easier, too, because Spanish is written as it's spoken. For example, in Spanish the vowel letter A is always read as "ah." In contrast, the English vowel letter A can represent several vowel sounds: "ei," "e," "ah," and so on.

The Spanish Alphabet

letter	pronunciation	letter	pronunciation
A	ah	Ñ	EH-nyeh
B	beh	O	oh
C	seh	P	pei
D	deh	Q	koo
E	eh	R	EH-reh
F	EF-eh	S	EH-seh
G	heh	T	teh
H	AH-cheh	U	oo
I	ee	V	veh, beh
J	HOH-tah	W	DOH-bleh veh,
K	kah		DOH-bleh beh
L	EH-leh	X	EH-kis
M	EH-meh	Y	ee GRIEH-gah
N	EH-neh	Z	ZEH-tah, SEH-tah

Pronunciation of Spanish Letters

letter	pronunciation	examples
A	"a" in "father"	mano (hand)
B	"b" in "box"	bella (pretty)
C	"c" in "call"	caja (box)
	"c" in "city"	cine (movies)
		(followed by "e" or "i")
D	"d" in "deck"	día (day)

Pronunciation of Spanish Letters *(continued)*

letter	pronunciation	examples
E	"e" in "pen"	pera (pear)
F	"f" in "fine"	fe (faith)
G	"g" in "go"	ganar (to win, earn)
	a hard "h"	gemelo (twin)
		(followed by "e" or "i")
H	mute, except in "ch"	hola (hello)
I	"i" in "seen"	listo (ready)
J	a hard "h"	justo (just, fair)
K	"k" in "karma"	koala (koala)
		(in words of foreign origin)
L	"l" in "lick"	lado (side)
M	"m" in "more"	mayo (May)
N	"n" in "nickel"	nada (nothing)
Ñ	similar to "ni" in "onion"	niño (baby, boy)
O	"o" in "more"	mosca (fly)
P	"p" in "open"	país (country)
Q	"k" in "king"	queso (cheese)
R	"tt" in "matter"	oro (gold)
S	"s" in "smart"	sonar (to ring)
T	"t" in "stay"	tamaño (size)
U	"oo" in "boot"	tuyo (yours)
V	"b" in "box"	vencer (to overcome)
W	"w" in "way"	waterpolo (waterpolo)
		(in words of foreign origin)
X	"x" in "taxes"	exilio (exile)
Y	like "y" in "yellow"	yo (I)
Z	like "s" in "smart"	zapato (shoe)

A Few Helpful Hints

Here are a few additional points to review:

- **B and V:** In many parts of the Spanish-speaking world, B and V are pronounced the same. At the beginning of the word or following M or N, they're pronounced like the "b" in "box." In all other cases, the Spanish B and V are actually modified to a soft "b" sound, with lips barely meeting. There's no equivalent of this sound in English, and you'll have to practice listening to it in Spanish and try to reproduce it.

- **D:** Pronunciation of D also depends on its place in the word. At the beginning or after L or N, it's pronounced like the "d" in "deck." In all other cases, it sounds more like the "th" in "mother."

- **X:** In words of American Indian origin, X may be pronounced as a hard "h" or "sh."

- **Y:** People in the Río de la Plata region (Argentina and Uruguay) pronounce Y (as well as the LL combination) like the "s" in "treasure."

- **Z:** Pronunciation of Z varies from country to country. In some parts of Spain, it's pronounced like "th" in "think." In a few areas, it's pronounced like the "z" in "zoo." In most of Latin America and Andalusia (Southern Spain), it's pronounced exactly the same as S.

Letter Combinations

To complete the guide to pronunciation, let's review the letter combinations used to represent additional sounds:

- **CH:** Just as in English, these two letters combine to form the sound of "ch" in "chin."
- **GU and QU:** Just as in English, "q" always comes in combination with "u," but the result is slightly different—the U remains silent. For example, que (that) is pronounced *keh*; quince (fifteen) is pronounced *KEEN-seh*. GU works the same way: guerra (war) is pronounced *GEH-rrah*. In GU words where the U is pronounced, it's written with two dots (an umlaut) to indicate the change in pronunciation. For example, vergüenza (shame), pronounced *behr-goo-EHN-sah*.
- **LL:** Generally, this combination serves to represent the sound "y" in "yellow." In Argentina and Uruguay, it is pronounced like the "s" in "measure."
- **RR:** This combination represents a long rolling "r" sound that does not have an equivalent in English. A single R at the beginning of a word also represents this sound.
- **UA:** In this vowel combination, the letter U becomes shorter, forming a sound similar to "w" in "war." For example, puerta (door) is pronounced *PWER-tah*.

Showing Stress

Because Spanish is written just like it sounds, spelling is rarely a problem. The only issue that may pose some difficulty is the use of the accent mark (´).

Accent marks aren't arbitrary. They're used to show which syllable should be stressed in words that don't follow the standard stress pattern. This pattern is easy to learn and can be described by two simple rules:

1. If a word ends in a vowel, N, or S, it is generally stressed on the second to last syllable. For example: *carta* (CAHR-tah), letter; *manchas* (MAHN-chahs), stains; *cantan* (CAHN-tahn), they sing.
2. If a word ends in a consonant other than N or S, it is generally stressed on the last syllable. For example: *merced* (mehr-CEHD), mercy; *cantar* (cahn-TAHR), to sing; *metal* (meh-TAHL), metal.

If the stress does not obey these rules, it must be signaled by adding an accent mark over the vowel in the correctly stressed syllable. For example, the word *útil*, useful, should be stressed on the last syllable, because it ends with an L. However, because the correct pronunciation of this word is *OO-teel* (and not *oo-TEEL*), an accent is placed over the vowel U. Following are a few other examples of words that require an accent mark because they do not follow the standard stress pattern.

fácil	easy
información	information
típico	typical
millón	million

Accent marks may also be used to distinguish words that are spelled and pronounced the same but have different meanings. For example, words like "who," "what," and "where" are spelled with an accent mark when they are used in questions, but they are spelled without the accent mark when they are used in the answer. For example:

¿Dónde está el almacén?
Where is the grocery store?
Está donde vive Carlos, en la calle Union.
It's where Carlos lives, on Union Street.

Here are a few common pairs of words that may be distinguished by the presence of the accent mark:

qué (what?)	que (what, that)
quién (who?)	quien (who, that)
dónde (where?)	donde (where, there)
cuándo (when?)	cuando (when, then)
cuánto (how much/many?)	cuanto (as much/many)
cómo (how?)	como (as, like)
sí (yes)	si (if)

continued

sólo (only)	solo (alone)
más (more)	mas (but)
mí (me)	mi (my)
tú (you)	tu (your)
él (he)	el (the)

Counting Off

Another basic skill is counting. Just as in English, Spanish numbers are organized by tens. To start counting, here is the first set, starting with zero:

0	cero	6	seis
1	uno	7	siete
2	dos	8	ocho
3	tres	9	nueve
4	cuatro	10	diez
5	cinco		

The next set of numbers includes the teens:

11	once	16	dieciséis
12	doce	17	diecisiete
13	trece	18	dieciocho
14	catorce	19	diecinueve
15	quince		

The numbers 20–29 are also written as one word:

20	veinte	25	veinticinco
21	veintiuno	26	veintiséis
22	veintidós	27	veintisiete
23	veintitrés	28	veintiocho
24	veinticuatro	29	veintinueve

Following 30, numbers are written as phrases: "thirty and one," "thirty and two," and so on. All you need to memorize are the numbers divisible by 10:

30	treinta	70	setenta
40	cuarenta	80	ochenta
50	cincuenta	90	noventa
60	sesenta		

Here are a few examples of numbers between 30 and 99:

32	treinta y dos	87	ochenta y siete
45	cuarenta y cinco	99	noventa y nueve
51	cincuenta y uno		

If you want to keep counting, the next number is *cien*, 100. Then, numbers continue up to 199 with *ciento* plus the rest of the number. Following are a few examples.

125	ciento veinticinco
146	ciento cuarenta y seis
189	ciento ochenta y nueve

The numbers from 200 to 999 work the same: You start with the hundreds, then add the rest of the number. For example, 348 is *trescientos cuarenta y ocho*.

200	doscientos	600	seiscientos
300	trescientos	700	setecientos
400	cuatrocientos	800	ochocientos
500	quinientos	900	novecientos

And don't forget that when these numbers are used to count nouns, the ending can change to feminine according to rules of agreement. For example: *cuatrocientas casas* (four hundred houses).

The higher you go, the pattern of forming the number by going from hundreds to tens to ones continues. For example, 1998 is *mil novecientos noventa y ocho*. Here's the rest of the vocabulary you might need to keep counting up:

1,000	mil
2,000	dos mil
1,000,000	millón
2,000,000	dos millones

For the Nth Time

Numbers used for counting (one, two, three) or as adjectives (one book, two books, three books) are known as cardinal numbers. But there's another group of numbers: ordinal numbers. Ordinal numbers don't deal with quantity—they serve to indicate the order of something: first, second, third, and so on. In English, all ordinal numbers following the first three end with –th, so they are easily recognized. In Spanish, the pattern is only slightly more complicated. You'll have to memorize the first ten:

first	primero	sixth	sexto
second	segundo	seventh	séptimo
third	tercero	eighth	octavo
fourth	cuarto	ninth	noveno
fifth	quinto	tenth	décimo

Starting with "eleventh," Spanish switches back to cardinal numbers, so "the eleventh hour" would be translated as *la hora once*.

The Structure of a Spanish Word

The most obvious way to improve your Spanish vocabulary is through memorization and practice. You cannot avoid memorizing words—it's the only sure way of increasing your vocabulary, and you won't be able to assimilate these words if you don't practice using them. However, additional strategies are available to you as well. For instance, by learning the meanings of common prefixes and suffixes, you'll be able to understand many more words than you have committed to memory. If you know that *cantar* means "to sing," and you know that *–ción* is a suffix equivalent to the English "–tion" and may be used to turn verbs into nouns, you might be able to guess that *canción* means "song."

A Spanish word may be made up of one or two parts—a lexeme (*lexema*) and/or a morpheme (*morfema*). The lexeme is the word's basic meaning, so it is generally the word's root. For example:

cocina	kitchen	cocineta	kitchenette
cocinar	to cook	precocinado	precooked
cocinero	cook, chef		

These five words share the root –cocin–, a lexeme that conveys the meaning of "cooking." The particles –a, –ar, –ero, –eta, pre–, and –ado (a prefix and five suffixes) may be called morphemes—they don't have a meaning on their own but they do add meaning when presented together with the root.

You can use lexemes and morphemes to your advantage. For example, once you understand that cocin is a root that has to do with cooking, you'll be able to guess the meaning of other words with the same lexeme, such as *cocido* (cooked) and *recocido* (overcooked)—as long as you are familiar with the prefix re– (over–) and suffix –ido (–ed).

Presenting the Prefix

A prefix (*prefijo*) is a morpheme that is attached to the front end of a word. In the word "prefix," for example, the prefix is "pre–." In Spanish prefijo, the prefix is the same: pre–.

The following list of Spanish prefixes is by no means complete, but it does include the more commonly used prefixes.

a– deprivation or negation; may have other meanings

ateísmo	atheism, rejection of theism
acabar	to end, to finish
atraer	to attract

ante– previously, beforehand, pre-, fore-

anteayer	day before yesterday
antemano	beforehand
antebrazo	forearm

anti– a prefix of opposition, anti-

antinatural	unnatural
antipatía	antipathy
antisudoral	antiperspirant

auto– self-, auto-, by oneself

autobiografía	autobiography, a biography of one's own life
autodefensa	self-defense
autorización	authorization

contra– a prefix of opposition

contracubierta	back cover
contragolpe	counter-blow
contrapelo	against the grain, the wrong way; literally "against the hair"

con– (also com– or co–) a prefix of addition or association

conmover	to move, to touch
consagrar	to consecrate
consorte	consort, accomplice
compadecer	to sympathize with
coautor	coauthor

de– (also des–) downward motion, separation, origin, opposite of the root meaning, emphasis

descender	to descend
denuncio	denunciation
derivar	to derive from
decolorado	discolored
demandar	to demand
desabrochar	to undo

en– (em– before "b" or "p") inside, on the interior; the prefix of connecting, enclosing

enlazar	to link
enmicar	to cover in plastic
embarazo	pregnancy

ex– outside of, further (over space or time); may not have a specific meaning

extraer	extract, draw
expansivo	expansive
explicar	to explain

extra– over, outside of, exceedingly

extrafino	superfine
extranjero	foreigner, outsider
extraño	strange

in– (im– before "b" or "p"; i– before "l" or "r") inside, on the interior; may carry a meaning of deprivation

incluir	to include
inacción	inaction
importante	important
iletrado	illiterate, uneducated

inter– between, among

internacional	international, among nations
interactivo	interactive
interesado	interested

para– with, to the side of, against

paradoja	paradox
parafrasear	to paraphrase
parasitario	parasitic

per– a prefix of intensity; may signify "badly"

perjurar	to perjure
pertinencia	relevance
pervivir	to survive

pre– prior to, priority, beforehand

pretexto	pretext
prevenido	cautious
previsión	foresight

pro– by or instead of, before, moving forward, denial or contradiction, in favor of

pronombre	pronoun
prólogo	prologue
propulsar	to drive, propel
proclamar	to proclaim
proponer	to propose

re– repetition, moving backwards, intensification, opposition

reeligir	to re-elect
recapacitar	to reconsider
recargar	to refill
rechazar	to refuse

sub– below; may also indicate inferiority

subarrendar	to sublet
subcutáneo	subcutaneous, under the skin
subempleo	underemployment

uni– one, alone

unido	united
universal	universal
unívoco	one to one

Following with the Suffix

A suffix (*sufijo*) is a morpheme that is attached to the end of a root. Suffixes often establish the word's grammatical role in the sentence—whether it's a noun, verb, or adjective: *divertirse* (to have fun), *diversión* (fun, a hobby), *divertido* (fun). The following list includes the more commonly used suffixes—knowing these suffixes can help you figure out the meanings of words you're not familiar with—or you can even try creating new words yourself.

–aje forms a noun from another noun; English equivalents are –ship and –age

aprendizaje	apprenticeship
caudillaje	leadership
kilometraje	"mileage" (for kilometers)

–ancia, –encia suffixes forms nouns; direct English equivalent is –ancy

corpulencia	stoutness
tolerancia	tolerance
violencia	violence

–anza forms a noun, often from a verb; English equivalents include –ance, –ion, and –ity

enseñanza	education
semejanza	similarity
venganza	vengeance

–ario a noun suffix that indicates a profession or place; English equivalents are –er, –ian, and –ry

bancario	banker
bibliotecario	librarian
campanario	bell tower

–arquía a suffix meaning "rule" or "government"; the English equivalent is –archy

anarquía	anarchy
jerarquía	hierarchy
monarquía	monarchy

–ble this suffix forms adjectives; it plays the same role in Spanish as it does in English

deseable	desirable
increíble	incredible
manejable	manageable

–cida/-cidio another noun suffix meaning "killing"; direct English equivalent is the suffix –cide

homicidio	homicide
insecticida	insecticide
suicidio	suicide

–ción a noun suffix; its direct English equivalent is –tion

información	information
presentación	presentation
culminación	culmination, end result

–dad this suffix often turns an adjective into a noun; the English equivalents are –ty and –hood

hermandad	brotherhood
lealdad	loyalty
verdad	truth

–ear a suffix that helps turn a noun into a verb

deletrear	to spell
parpadear	to blink
pasear	to stroll, take a walk

–ense a suffix that is added to a country's name to create the adjective of nationality

canadiense	Canadian
costarriquence	Costa Rican
rioplatense	from the Rio Plata region in South America

–ería a noun suffix indicating a place (often a shop)

lavandería	laundromat
panadería	bakery
zapatería	shoe store

–ero/–era may indicate a profession or role; English equivalents include –er and –or

ingeniero	engineer
traicionero	traitor
portero	doorman

–esa/–iz/–isa indicates profession in the feminine; English equivalent is –ess

actriz	actress
duquesa	duchess
poetisa	poetess

–eza a suffix used to turn an adjective into a noun; an English equivalent is –ty

belleza	beauty
pureza	purity
riqueza	riches, wealth

–icio/–icia a noun suffix; English equivalent is –ice

avaricia	avarice
novicio	novice
justicia	justice

–ificar a suffix that forms verbs and means "turn into"; English equivalent is –ify

dignificar	to dignify
dosificar	to measure out (dose)
significar	to mean

–ismo a noun suffix that refers to a "theory" or "ideology";
English equivalent is –ism

comunismo	communism
racismo	racism
realismo	realism

–ista a noun suffix that is often used to indicate profession or
role; English equivalent is –ist

comunista	communist
dentista	dentist
pianista	pianist

–izo an adjective suffix that connotes uncertainty or
incompleteness of a quality (English equivalent is –ish); signals
what something is made of

cobrizo	coppery
pajizo	made of straw
rojizo	reddish

–mente a common suffix used to turn an adjective into an
adverb; English equivalent is –ly

claramente	clearly
obviamente	obviously
precisamente	precisely

–or a noun suffix that is often used to represent a profession or role; English equivalents include –er and –or

director	director, editor, headmaster, manager
jugador	player
pintor	painter

–oso a suffix you can use to turn a noun into an adjective; English equivalent is –ous

jugoso	juicy
maravilloso	marvelous
peligroso	dangerous

–tud a noun suffix that often refers to a state of being; English equivalent is –ude

actitud	attitude
latitud	latitude
solicitud	solicitude

Diminutives and Augmentatives

There are two groups of suffixes that deserve special attention—they are the suffixes that form diminutives and augmentatives. These are suffixes that can be added to a whole range of words and the resulting words don't require a dictionary definition—the suffixes don't change the word's meaning, they simply signal additional information like size or the speaker's emotional attitude.

Diminutive—Small

"Diminutive" means "small"; diminutive suffixes indicate small size, cuteness, or the attitude of endearment. The word *caja* means "box"; *cajita* is a little box, perhaps one of those ring boxes. *Perro* is a dog; *perrito* is "doggy." As you can see, using a diminutive suffix can allow you to be more descriptive without resorting to adjectives.

The most versatile diminutive suffix in Spanish is –ito and its conjugated forms, –ita, –itos, and –itas: *conejito* (little bunny), *abuelita* (granny), *chiquitos* (little/cute boys), *abejitas* (little/cute bees). Following are a few other diminutive suffixes commonly used in Spanish.

–cito (–cita)	ratoncito	little mouse
–illo (–illa)	chiquillo	little boy
–zuelo (–zuela)	jovenzuelo	youth

You can take almost any noun and give it a diminutive suffix. Even adjectives and, to a lesser extent, adverbs can take on diminutive endings: *viejito* (old), *rapidito* (quickly). However, be aware that diminutives are often considered "slangy" and should not be overused in writing or in formal speech.

Augmentative—Large

The word "augmentative" means "enlarging" (to augment is to enlarge). Augmentatives are similar to diminutives, except that their endings carry a different tone—they indicate large size or the attitude of toughness or importance. For example, *hombre* is "man," but add the augmentative suffix –ón, and the result is *hombrón*, "tough guy." Here's a list of common augmentative suffixes:

–ote (–ota)	grandote	very big
–ón (–ona)	barracón	a big hut
–azo (–aza)	buenazo	really good

Recognizing Cognates

Another way to improve your vocabulary is by learning how to recognize cognates—word pairs that look alike or are very similar in English and in Spanish. True cognates are cognates that also share a common or very similar meaning. For example, compare "attention" and *atención*—these two words have a similar spelling and share a similar meaning. And *exterior* is identical to the English "exterior."

In the case of some Spanish cognates, it's easy to see what they could mean in English. For example, if you encounter the word *cliente*, you'll likely be able to guess that it's a cognate of "client." Likewise, *imposible* looks very much like "impossible," though it's pronounced slightly differently (the "e" isn't silent, and the accent is on the "si" syllable).

Other cognate pairs aren't as obvious, however, and you'll need to practice guessing to be able to figure out the correct meaning. For example, it may not be immediately clear that *traducción* is the Spanish cognate of "translation" or that *estudiar* is a cognate for "to study."

Furthermore, some simple Spanish words have English cognates that we would consider old-fashioned words or even "vocabulary" words. Compare the following:

aumentar	to augment (to increase)
discordia	discord (disagreement)
escolástico	scholastic (academic, scholarly)
penúltimo	penultimate (second to last)
serpiente	serpent (snake)

One important benefit of learning these cognates is that you'll also improve your English vocabulary.

Commonly Misused Cognates

Although paying attention is to your advantage, it's important to keep in mind that not all cognates are true cognates—that is, not all cognates actually have a common or similar meaning in English and Spanish. Many a student of Spanish has been mortified to learn that *embarazada* means "pregnant" and not "embarrassed," as may be concluded.

"Embarrassed" and *embarazada* are just one pair of false cognates. The tables on the following pages list a few others.

Spanish	Correct English Translation	False Cognate	Correct Spanish Translation
asistir	to attend	to assist	ayudar
atender	to serve	to attend	asistir
billón	trillion	billion	mil millones
campo	field, countryside	camp	campamento, facción
chocar	to crash	to choke	ahogar, sofocar
colegio	school	college	escuela universitaria, universidad
compromiso	obligation, compromise	commitment	arreglo, solución
constiparse	to catch a cold	to be constipated	estar extreñido
desgracia	misfortune	disgrace	deshonra
educado	well-mannered, polite	educated	culto
embarazada	pregnant	embarrassed	avergonzado
emocionante	thrilling, moving	emotional	emocional
éxito	success	exit	salida
fábrica	factory	fabric	tela

(continued)

Spanish	Correct English Translation	False Cognate	Correct Spanish Translation (*continued*)
firma	signature	firm	compañía
idioma	language	idiom	modismo
largo	long	large	grande
librería	bookstore	library	biblioteca
molestar	to bother	to molest	agredir sexualmente
pretender	to try	to pretend	fingir, (similar to hope to achieve)
raro	strange	rare	excepcional, poco común
realizar	to actualize	to realize	darse cuenta
ropa	clothing	rope	cuerda
sano	healthy	sane	cuerdo, sabio
sensible	sensitive	sensible	razonable, sensato
sopa	soup	soap	jabón
suceso	event	success	éxito
vaso	drinking glass	vase	jarrón

02 / Building Your Vocabulary

What Time Is It?

Okay, so you've already learned your numbers in Spanish. Now what? One of the handy things you can do with this newfound knowledge is telling time, or more likely, understanding the answer when you ask a Spanish-speaker what time it is. Remember that you need to use the verb *ser* (which you'll learn to conjugate in the grammar chapter) when talking about time.

Asking *¿Qué hora es?* (What time is it?) literally means, "What hour is it?" That means that the verb in the answer needs to agree with the number of hours that it is:

Es la una.
It's one o'clock.
Son las dos.
It's two o'clock.

It's also common for people to use the expression *¿Qué horas son?* This is equally correct. Note also that the hour of day is a feminine noun and so takes the feminine article *la*.

Time of Day
Here are some phrases for telling the time of day:

It's noon.	It's 7:25.
Es el mediodía.	*Son las siete y veinticinco.*
It's midnight.	It's 8:30.
Es la medianoche.	*Son las ocho y media.*
It's 1:00.	It's 9:35.
Es la una.	*Son las diez menos veinticinco.*
It's 3:05.	It's 12:50.
Son las tres y cinco.	*Es la una menos diez.*

▶ Other Time Phrases

in the morning	por la mañana
in the afternoon	por la tarde
in the evening	por la noche
At what time?	¿A qué hora?
Since what time?	¿Desde qué hora?
Since two.	Desde las dos.
A half-hour ago.	Hace media hora.
a second	un segundo
a minute	un minuto
an hour	una hora

Days of the Week, Months of the Year

Ah, vacation. Who cares what day of the week it is? Well, it'll come in handy for remembering when you're supposed to get back on that plane.

▶ Days of the Week

day	día
Sunday	domingo
Monday	lunes
Tuesday	martes
Wednesday	miércoles
Thursday	jueves
Friday	viernes
Saturday	sábado

▶ Months of the Year

month	mes
January	enero
February	febrero
March	marzo
April	abril
May	mayo
June	junio
July	julio
August	agosto
September	septiembre
October	octubre
November	noviembre
December	diciembre

▶ **Seasons**

season	la estación
winter	el invierno
spring	la primavera
summer	el verano
fall	el otoño

How's the Weather?

Can't think of anything to say to that friendly person standing next to you? No matter the language, there's always that old stand-by: the weather. To talk about the weather, you'll use the verbs *hacer*, "to do" or "to make," and *estar*. You'll also use the word *hay*, an adverbial expression that means "there is/are."

HACER: to do, to make

yo hago	nosotros hacemos
tú haces	vosotros hacéis
él, ella, usted hace	ellos, ellas, ustedes hacen

The literal translations for weather expressions in Spanish are a bit odd to the ear of the English-speaker. The equivalent of "It's cold" is *Hace frío* in Spanish, which literally means "It makes cold."

How's the weather?   It's cool.
¿Qué tiempo hace?   *Hace fresco./Está fresco.*
It's cold.   It's windy.
Hace frío.   *Hay viento./Está ventoso.*

It's bad weather.	It's cloudy.
Hace mal tiempo.	*Está nublado.*
It's hot.	It's raining.
Hace calor.	*Está lloviendo.*
It's humid.	There's lightning.
Hay humedad.	*Hay relámpagos.*
It's sunny.	There's thunder.
Hace sol.	*Hay truenos.*
It's nice weather.	It's snowing.
Hace buen tiempo.	*Está nevando.*

The key to learning any skill is to use it. Now that you know how to talk about the weather, why not get out there and practice what you've learned?

Physical Characteristics

¿Cómo te ves? What do you look like? To answer, you can use the verb *ser* (to be) and *tener* (to have), plus a series of adjectives that describe your stature, hair and eye color, and so on. You will learn how to conjugate these verbs in the grammar chapter, but for now, you can use these helpful phrases. For example:

> Yo soy alto y delgado. Tengo el pelo corto de color castaño y los ojos azules.
> *I am tall and thin. I have chestnut-colored hair and blue eyes.*

Here's some useful vocabulary for describing yourself and others.

▶ Height and Size

alto	tall
bajo	short
mediano	medium
gordo, corpulento	fat
delgado, flaco	thin

▶ Hair

corto	short
largo	long
liso	straight
rizado	curly
rubio	blond
pelirrojo	red
castaño	chestnut-colored
moreno	brown, dark brown
negro	black
canoso	gray

▶ Eyes

azul	blue
pardo, marrón	brown
negro	black
verde	green
color de avellana	hazel
claro	light
oscuro	dark

▶ Other Adjectives

joven	young
viejo	old
bonito	pretty
bello	beautiful
guapo	handsome
feo	ugly
interesante	interesting
simpático	nice

Family Relations

La familia (the family) plays an important part in the lives of the people living around the Spanish world. To get all the relationships straight, here's some relevant vocabulary:

▶ Relatives

madre	mother
padre	father
padres	parents
marido, esposo	husband
esposa, mujer	wife
hijo, hija	son, daughter
hermano, hermana	brother, sister
gemelo, mellizo	twin
abuelo, abuela	grandfather, grandmother
nieto, nieta	grandson, granddaughter
tío, tía	uncle, aunt
sobrino, sobrina	nephew, niece

Relatives *(continued)*

primo	cousin
suegro, suegra	father-in-law, mother-in-law
yerno	son-in-law
nuera	daughter-in-law
padrino	godfather
madrina	godmother
de acogida	foster

Practice the vocabulary by reviewing your family tree. For example:

Me llamo Jorge. Soy ingeniero. Mis padres son Juan y Renata. Mi padre es médico; mi madre es enfermera. Yo estoy casado con María. Ella es una actriz de teatro. Mi esposa y yo tenemos dos hijos: Elena y Daniel. Elena es estudiante en la escuela secundaria. Daniel asiste a la universidad. También tengo una hermana, Marta. Ella vive en Colombia. Trabaja en un banco. Marta tiene un hijo, Cristóbal. A Elena y Daniel les gusta visitar a su tía y a sus primos en Colombia.

How much were you able to understand? Here's the translation:

My name is Jorge. I'm an engineer. My parents are Juan and Renata. My father is a doctor; my mother is a nurse. I am married to María. She is

*a theater actress. My wife and I have two kids:
Elena and Daniel. Elena is a high school student.
Daniel goes to college. I also have a sister, Marta.
She lives in Colombia. She works at a bank. Marta
has a son, Cristóbal. Elena and Daniel like to visit
their aunt and cousins in Colombia.*

Now, how about trying to describe your own family? What are they like?

Back to School

Whether you're in high school, college, or just taking a class to learn some Spanish, you can really impress your instructor if you are comfortable with some classroom vocabulary. You probably know a lot of these terms—review the ones you do know and commit to memory the vocabulary you haven't encountered before.

▶ In the Classroom

estudiante	student
profesor, profesora	high school teacher
maestro	elementary school teacher
catedrático	professor
pluma, bolígrafo	pen
lápiz	pencil
goma de borrar	pencil eraser
papel	paper
cuaderno	notebook

▶ In the Classroom (continued)

libro	book
carpeta	folder
mochila	backpack
pizarra	board
tiza	chalk
borrador	board eraser
reloj	clock, watch
silla	chair
escritorio	desk
cartel	poster
cesta	wastebasket

If your Spanish classes are conducted in Spanish, it'll help to know some basic phrases as well. Here are a few to get you started:

¿Cómo se dice "grades" en castellano?
How do you say "grades" in Spanish?
Señor Blanco, ¿puede usted repetir su pregunta, por favor?
Mr. White, can you please repeat your question?
¿Cuándo tendremos el examen final?
When are we having the final exam?
No entiendo cómo conjugar el verbo "ser". Explíquemelo, por favor.
I don't know how to conjugate the verb ser. Please explain it to me.
¿Podemos usar el diccionario durante la prueba?
Can we use the dictionary during the quiz?
¿Puedo ir al baño, por favor?
May I please go to the bathroom?

Getting Around

For coming, going, traveling, and wandering, you'll need to add some new verbs of motion to your vocabulary arsenal. First is the verb *ir*, "to go." Again, you will learn how to conjugate this verb and others in Chapter 3, but here are some useful tips on the verb. Just like the verbs *ser* and *estar*, *ir* is used in conversation so often that you'll learn it in no time.

IR: to go

yo voy	*nosotros vamos*
tú vas	*vosotros vais*
él, ella, usted va	*ellos, ellas, ustedes van*

Ir is a versatile verb that can be used in several ways. For example, *ir* is the verb you need to indicate your destination:

Voy a Madrid.
I'm going to Madrid.
Sara va al hotel.
Sara goes to the hotel.
Los niños van a la escuela.
The children go to school.

You can also use the verb *ir* to talk about what you're going to do. Combine the conjugated form of *ir* with the preposition *a* (to) and the infinitive form of another verb, and you've got a way to express the future.

Voy a salir a las ocho.
I'm going to leave at eight.
Juan va a leer.
Juan is going to read.
Vamos a caminar juntos.
We are going to walk together.

Here are some more verbs you can use when talking about coming and going:

- *andar*: to walk
- *caminar*: to walk
- *conducir*: to drive
- *tomar*: to take
- *viajar*: to travel

ANDAR: to walk

yo ando	*nosotros andamos*
tú andas	*vosotros andáis*
él, ella, usted anda	*ellos, ellas, ustedes andan*

Here is how you can use the verb *andar*:

Yo ando al museo.
I walk to the museum.
Carla y yo andamos juntos.
Carla and I walk together.
Las niñas andan en bicicleta.
The girls ride bicycles.

Caught you off guard with that last example? *Andar* is most often translated as "to walk," but this verb can also be used to mean "to go" or "to ride." Don't worry! The context it's used in will pretty much always make the meaning perfectly clear.

CAMINAR: to walk

yo camino	nosotros caminamos
tú caminas	vosotros camináis
él, ella, usted camina	ellos, ellas, ustedes caminan

The verb *caminar* is a synonym of *andar*. Here are a few examples of how it might be used:

En Miami caminamos por la playa.
We walk on the beach in Miami.
Yo prefiero caminar por la tarde.
I prefer walking in the afternoon.

In the last example, the first-person form of *preferir* (to prefer) was combined with the infinitive form of *caminar*—a simple way to express more complex thoughts.

CONDUCIR: to drive

yo conduzco	nosotros conducimos
tú conduces	vosotros conducís
él, ella, usted conduce	ellos, ellas, ustedes conducen

Use *conducir* to refer to driving a vehicle:

Tú conduces muy bien.
You drive very well.
Es difícil conducir en una cuidad nueva.
It's difficult to drive in a new city.

TOMAR: to take

yo tomo	nosotros tomamos
tú tomas	vosotros tomáis
él, ella, usted toma	ellos, ellas, ustedes toman

The verb *tomar* may be used to mean "take" in the sense of taking something, or it may indicate the "taking" of food or drink (it's used more frequently to mean "to drink"):

Tomamos un taxi al restaurante.
We take a taxi to the restaurant.
Yo nunca tomo agua fría.
I never drink cold water.

To say someone is "*tomado*" is to say they're drunk. If someone says, "*Yo no tomo*" they are telling you they don't drink alcohol.

VIAJAR: to travel

yo viajo	nosotros viajamos
tú viajas	vosotros viajáis
él, ella, usted viaja	ellos, ellas, ustedes viajan

The use of *viajar* is straightforward:

Ellos viajan juntos a España.
They travel to Spain together.
¿Cúando vas a viajar conmigo?
When are you going to travel with me?

Where Am I?

Finding your way is a lot easier if you know how to ask for directions. It's even easier if you understand the response!

Where is . . . ?
¿Dónde está . . . ?
I'm going to . . .
Voy a . . .
How do I get to . . . from here?
¿Cómo voy a . . . de aquí?
Can you help me?
¿Puede ayudarme?
Is it far?
¿Es lejos?
Can I walk from here to there?
¿Puedo caminar de aquí hasta allá?

Where is the nearest bus stop?
¿Dónde está la parada de autobús más cercana?
Where can I buy a ticket?
¿Dónde puedo comprar un billete?
Can you show it to me on this map?
¿Puede enseñármelo en esta mapa?

▶ Locations

American Embassy	la embajada americana
metro station	la estación de metro
train station	la estación de trenes
block	la manzana
building	el edificio
sidewalk	la acera
street	la calle
street corner	la esquina

▶ Prepositions of Location

across from	en frente a
ahead	más adelante
behind	detrás de
near	cerca
next to	al lado de
far	lejos

▶ Directions

east	este
left	izquierda
north	norte

▶ Directions (continued)

right	derecha
south	sur
straight	derecho
west	oeste

▶ A Few Verbs of Command

continue	siga
take	tome
turn	doble
walk	camine
cross	cruce
go back	vuelva
go down	baje
go past	pase
go up	suba

Transportation

If the distance from Point A to Point B is farther than your feet can carry you, you'll need to hop on one form of transportation or another. Here are the phrases and terms you'll need to get you where you're going.

How much is the fare?
¿Cuánto es la tarifa?
Is this seat taken?
¿Está ocupado este asiento?
What is the next stop?
¿Cuál es la próxima parada?

Excuse me. I'm getting off here.
Con permiso. Bajo aquí.

▶ Take a Cab

fare	el precio del viaje
taxi	el taxi
taxi driver	el taxista
taxi stand	la parada de taxis
tip	la propina

Here are a few additional phrases for communicating with cabbies:

Stop here.
Pare aquí.
Please wait for me.
Espéreme, por favor.
Can you please open the trunk?
¿Puede abrir el maletero, por favor?
How much do I owe you?
¿Cuánto le debo?

▶ Ride the Subway

subway	el metro
ticket machine	la máquina de billetes
fare	la tarifa
metro station	la estación de metro
platform	el andén

Can I connect to the . . . line here?
¿Puedo cambiar a la línea . . . aquí?
Which line goes to . . . ?
¿Cuál línea va a . . . ?

▶ Take the Bus

bus	el autobús
bus driver	el conductor
fare	la tarifa
bus stop	la parada de autobús
bus station	la estación de autobús
ticket	el billete

▶ In the Train

train station	la estación de trenes
schedule	el horario
conductor	el cobrador
first class ticket	el billete de primera clase
second class ticket	el billete de segunda clase
smoking compartment	el compartimiento para fumadores
non-smoking compartment	el compartimiento para no fumadores
sleeper compartment	el compartimiento con literas
platform	el andén
ticket	el billete
ticket window	la taquilla
one-way ticket	el billete sencillo
round-trip ticket	el billete de ida y vuelta

▶ **Renting a Car**

car	el coche
to rent	alquilar
car rental	el alquiler de coches
driver's license	el carné de conducir
breakdown	la avería
car accident	el choque
traffic	el tráfico
dent	la abolladura
gasoline	la gasolina
excess kilometers	los kilómetros de exceso
oil	el aceite
directions	las señas
insurance	el seguro
highway	la carretera
street	la calle
toll	el peaje
bridge	el puente

Time to Eat!

With all this traipsing about town, you've probably worked up quite an appetite. Now it's time to learn food vocabulary words so you can find what you want (and maybe, more importantly, what you don't want) on a menu. We wouldn't want you to end up with a tortilla made with pigs' brains (yes, you can really get that in Spain!) unless that's what you want to order.

You may find the following words useful as you're trying to order food from a menu, or as you shop for

ingredients at a local supermarket, grocery store, or
outdoor market. To make the tables more manageable,
they are organized by food type.

▶ Adjectives to Describe Your Meal

fresh	fresca
sweet	dulce
sour	agrio
bland	soso
spicy	picante
hot	caliente
cold	frío

▶ Methods of Preparation

baked	al horno
grilled	a la parrilla
roasted	asado
fried	frito
sautéed	salteado
toasted	tostado
raw	crudo
rare	poco cocido
medium	a término medio
well-done	bien cocido
steamed	al vapor
chopped	picado
burned	quemado

▶ General Food Groups

fish	el pescado
shellfish	el marisco
chocolate	el chocolate
fat	la grasa
dairy	los productos lácteos
vegetable	la verdura
fruit	la fruta
grains	los cereales
bread	el pan
meat	la carne
poultry	las aves de corral
soup	la sopa
salad	la ensalada
sandwich (on a roll)	el bocadillo
sandwich (on sliced bread)	el sándwich

▶ Fruit

apple	la manzana
apricot	el albaricoque
banana	la banana
blueberry	el mirtilo
cherry	la cereza
coconut	el coco
date	el dátil
fig	el higo
grape	la uva

▶ Fruit *(continued)*

grapefruit	el pomelo
guava	la guayaba
lemon	el limón
lime	la lima
melon	el melón
nectarine	la nectarina
orange	la naranja
peach	el durazno/el melocotón
pear	la pera
pineapple	el ananá/la piña
plantain	el plátano
plum	la ciruela
prune	la ciruela pasa
raisin	la pasa de uva
raspberry	la frambuesa
strawberry	la fresa
watermelon	la sandía

▶ Vegetables

asparagus	los espárragos
artichoke	la alcachofa
avocado	el aguacate
beans	los frijoles
beet	la remolacha
broccoli	el brécol
cabbage	la col
carrot	la zanahoria
cauliflower	la coliflor

▶ **Vegetables** *(continued)*

celery	el apio
chickpeas	los garbanzos
corn	el maíz
cucumber	el pepino
eggplant	la berenjena
green beans	las judías
kale	la rizada
lentils	las lentejas
lettuce	la lechuga
mushroom	el champiñon
onion	la cebolla
peas	los guisantes
pepper	el pimiento
potato	la papa
spinach	la espinaca
squash	la calabaza
sweet potato	la batata/el boniato
tomato	el tomate
zucchini	el calabacín

▶ **Dairy**

butter	la mantequilla
cheese	el queso
cream	la nata
egg	el huevo
ice cream	el helado
milk	la leche
yogurt	el yogur

▶ Grains

bran	el salvado
breakfast cereal	el cereal del desayuno
flour	la harina
oatmeal	los copos de avena
oats	la avena
rice	el arroz
wheat	el trigo

▶ Bread

dinner roll	el bollo
loaf of bread	la barra de pan
slice of bread	la rebanada de pan
toast	el pan tostado
whole wheat bread	el pan integral

▶ Meat and Poultry

beef	la carne de vaca o de res
cutlet	la chuleta
filet mignon	el lomo fino
goat	el chivo
ham	el jamón
hamburger	la hamburguesa
hot dog	la salchicha
lamb	la carne de cordero
liver	el hígado
pork	la carne de cerdo

▶ Meat and Poultry *(continued)*

roast beef	el rosbíf
sausage	el chorizo
steak	el bistec
veal	la carne de ternera
chicken	el pollo
duck	el pato
turkey	el pavo

▶ Fish and Shellfish

anchovy	la anchoa
bass	la merluza
clam	la almeja
cod	el bacalao
crab	el cangrejo
eel	la anguila
obster	la langosta
mussel	el mejillón
oyster	la ostra
salmon	el salmón
scallops	las conchas de peregrino
shark	el tiburón
shrimp	las gambas
sole	el lenguado
swordfish	el pez espada
trout	la trucha
tuna	el atún

▶ Dessert

cake	la torta
cookie	la galleta
ice cream	el helado
pie	el pastel
pudding	el pudín
rice pudding	el arroz con leche

▶ Beverages

alcohol	el alcohol
beer	la cerveza
champagne	el champán
coffee	el café
hot chocolate	el chocolate
juice	el jugo
milk	la leche
milk shake	el batido
mineral water	el agua mineral
rum	el ron
sherry	el jerez
soda	la gaseosa
tea	el té
water	el agua
carbonated water	el agua con gas
noncarbonated water	el agua sin gas
wine	el vino

You'll find the following set of verbs especially helpful when ordering in a restaurant, shopping in a grocery store, or just talking about your culinary likes and dislikes:

- *comer*: to eat
- *beber*: to drink
- *querer*: to want
- *necesitar*: to need
- *gustar*: to like, to be pleasing to

And don't forget about *tomar*, which means "to take" but is also used to mean "to drink" and, less often, "to eat." You'll learn more about conjugating these verbs later, but for now, here are some common uses you may run into in the food world!

COMER: to eat

yo como	nosotros comemos
tú comes	vosotros coméis
él, ella, usted come	ellos, ellas, ustedes comen

Armed with the verb *comer*, you can tell the waiter that you don't eat certain foods. For example:

Yo no como carne.
I don't eat meat.
Juan Carlos siempre come almuerzo.
Juan Carlos always eats lunch.

BEBER: to drink

yo bebo	nosotros bebemos
tú bebes	vosotros bebéis
él, ella, usted bebe	ellos, ellas, ustedes beben

Beber is used to talk about drinking, although sometimes *tomar* is used instead:

La niña bebe leche.
The girl drinks milk.
Ellos beben gaseosa cuando comen pizza.
They drink soda when they eat pizza.
Billy toma su té en el patio.
Billy drinks his tea on the patio.

QUERER: to want

yo quiero	nosotros queremos
tú quieres	vosotros queréis
él, ella, usted quiere	ellos, ellas, ustedes quieren

In Spanish, the verb *querer* is used to mean "want" in the sense of liking or needing something:

¿Qué queréis comer?
What would you like to eat?
¿Quieres más agua?
Do you want more water?

Also note that to ask for what you would like, you need to use the imperfect subjunctive form of *querer*:

QUERER in Imperfect Subjunctive

yo quisiera	nosotros quisiéramos
tú quisieras	vosotros quisierais
él, ella, usted quisiera	ellos, ellas, ustedes quisieran

Using *querer* in the imperfect subjunctive is a polite way of asking for something. For example:

Quisiera un vaso de agua, por favor.
I would like a glass of water, please.
Quisiéramos ver la carta, por favor.
We would like to see the menu, please.

NECESITAR: to need

yo necesito	nosotros necesitamos
tú necesitas	vosotros necesitáis
él, ella, usted necesita	ellos, ellas, ustedes necesitan

When you need something, don't be afraid to say it with *necesitar*:

Necesito más pan, por favor.
I need more bread, please.
Los niños necesitan comer menos dulces.
The children need to eat fewer sweets.

Likes and Dislikes

The verb *gustar* is a little different from other verbs. In English, you say "I like something." In Spanish, however, the expression is *me gusta*—literally, "to me, it is pleasing." The difference is that the subject in the Spanish sentence isn't "I"—it's what you like!

If the "liked" object is singular, use *gusta* (third person singular form). If the object is plural, use *gustan* (third person plural form).

GUSTAR: equivalent of "to like"

me gusta(n)	nos gusta(n)
te gusta(n)	os gusta(n)
le gusta(n)	les gusta(n)

El café te gusta.
You like coffee. (Literally, "Coffee is pleasing to you.")
No nos gusta el pan.
We don't like bread.

▶ Restaurant Vocabulary

waiter/waitress	el/la camarero/a
check	la cuenta
table	la mesa
tablecloth	el mantel
place setting	los cubiertos
fork	el tenedor
knife	el cuchillo
spoon	la cuchara

▶ Restaurant Vocabulary *(continued)*

teaspoon	la cucharita
cup	la taza
glass	el vaso
wine glass	la copa de vino
plate	el plato
bowl	el tazón
napkin	la servilleta
restroom	los baños
tip	la propina
chef	el/la cocinero/a
manager	el/la gerente
entrée	el plato principal
dessert	el postre
snack	la merienda
appetizer	el aperitivo
breakfast	el desayuno
lunch	el almuerzo
dinner	la cena

Below you will find some common Spanish foods you'll probably see on your menu!

▶ On the Menu

carta, menú	menu
antojito	appetizer
ensalada	salad
sopa	soup
caldo	broth

▶ On the Menu *(continued)*

pescado	fish
mariscos	seafood
ave	poultry
carne	meat
salsa	sauce
legumbres	vegetables or legume
vegetales	green vegetables
pan	bread
postre	dessert
bebida	drink
ceviche	fish or seafood cured in lemon juice
empanada	savory stuffed pastry (usually stuffed with meat)
chuleta	(pork) chop
bistec	(beef) steak
hígado	liver
salchicha	pork sausage
salpicón	cold non-vegetable salad (usually with seafood)
chorizo	pork sausage
lomo de cerdo	pork loin
tocino	salted pork
pozole	hominy stew
tortilla española	Spanish potato omelette
croqueta	croquette
mofongo	mashed plantains (often with seafood)

▶ **On the Menu** *(continued)*

al ajillo	in garlic sauce
al horno	baked
arroz con frijoles	rice and beans
paella	a saffron rice dish (usually prepared with seafood)
arepa	corn pancake
tamales	corn patties (usually with minced meat)
yucca	a root vegetable similar to a potato
tostones	savory fried plantains
maduros	sweet (ripe) fried plantains
arroz con leche	rice pudding
batido	milk shake
helado	ice cream
flan	custard
buñuelo	fritter
sangría	a mix of wine and fruit juices
café	coffee
agua	water
jugo	juice

Food Shopping

If you've decided to skip the restaurant and head out to the local shops to buy groceries, you'll need to figure out where the shops are. And to do that, you have to know what they're called in Spanish.

▶ Types of Food Stores

grocery store	el colmado
butcher shop	la carnicería
bakery	la panadería
delicatessen	la salchichonería
supermarket	el supermercado
pastry shop	la pastelería
fish shop	la pescadería
ice cream shop	la heladería

▶ How Much Do You Want?

a little bit	un poco
a lot	mucho
a bite of	un pincho de
an order of	una ración de
a box of	una caja de
a bag of	una bolsa de
a can of	una lata de
a jar of	un tarro de
a bottle of	una botella de
a sack of	un saco de

Now that you have a working vocabulary, it's time for an introduction to Spanish grammar!

03 / Grammar

AS YOU BEGIN to study Spanish grammar, it might be helpful to start by getting an overview of grammar, and how it works in English as well as in Spanish. Remember, you're not starting from scratch. You already know a lot about grammar because you can speak and write in English.

Despite how it might seem, Spanish grammar and English grammar aren't all that different. Although English isn't a Romance language, it was heavily influenced by one. England hadn't been a part of the Roman Empire for long, so Latin didn't really get a chance to spread to the local populations. However, in 1066, when French-speaking Normans invaded England and took control, their language merged with Old English, a Germanic tongue, to form what today we can recognize as English.

Moreover, during the Middle Ages and up to the twentieth century, education in Britain included the study of Latin, which might explain why English is now full of long vocabulary words like "excoriate," "penultimate," and "prevaricate" (or, more simply, "criticize," "next to the last," and "lie").

Blueprint of a Sentence

To begin, let's first look at the structure of the sentence and how it works and then look at the parts of speech that may make up the sentence. Each sentence is made up of two main parts: subject and predicate. Think of the subject as the hero of the sentence. It's the word or phrase that does the action or carries the description. The predicate is the rest—the action. Generally, but not always, the subject will come before the predicate.

subject	predicate
My friends and I	go to the movies every Friday.
The girl that I had seen last Friday	isn't at home today.
Many students	take Spanish in the morning.
We	like it.

Note that the subject answers the question "who or what?" and the predicate answers what the subject is or does. Take the sentence, "We like it." Who likes it? We do—so we is the subject. We do what? We like it—here, "like it" is the predicate. Who isn't at home today? The girl that I had seen last Friday. The girl that I had seen last Friday isn't what? She isn't at home today.

The predicate always includes a verb or verb phrase and may also include a complement. In the previous example, the predicate "like it" is made up of the verb "like" and the complement "it". Some verbs can stand alone, without a complement; others cannot.

Parts of Speech

Subjects and predicates can be further broken down into parts of speech. Spanish and English grammar identifies eight major elements:

noun	sustantivo
pronoun	pronombre
adjective	adjetivo
verb	verbo
adverb	adverbio
preposition	preposición
conjunction	conjunción
interjection	interjección

Even if you can't tell the difference between these terms, when you speak you intuitively know which are which and how they should be used. The following sections will define these parts of speech so that as you start learning Spanish grammar, these words will not intimidate you.

Name a Noun

Let's start with nouns. A noun may be any of the following.

Thing:

computadora (computer)
escritorio (desk)
bolígrafo (pen)

Place:

playa (beach)
ciudad (city)
mundo (world)

Person:

madre (mother)
Carlos (boy's name)
estudiante (student)

Concept:

verdad (truth)
conciencia (awareness)
conducta (behavior)

If you can match up a word with an article (*the*, *a*, or *an*), it's definitely a noun, but not all nouns can have one: proper names like *John* and *Spain* don't take on articles in English.

A Pro with Pronouns

The first thing to remember about pronouns is that they are replacements for nouns or noun phrases. When you keep talking about the same noun, you might get sick of constantly repeating it, so you resort to a pronoun:

John went home. He went home.
Give James a drink. Give him a drink. Give it to him.
Rita's car is red. Her car is red.
I will do it myself.

In these examples, "he," "him," "it," "her," and "myself" are personal pronouns. That is, they work to replace specific nouns. Here's how personal pronouns are categorized: Subject pronouns replace the subject of the sentence. Object pronouns replace the object of the verb (whether it's a noun or a phrase). Possessive pronouns show ownership. Reflexive pronouns signal that the subject and the object are one and the same.

▶ Subject Pronouns

singular	plural
yo (I)	nosotros, nosotras (we)
tú (you, informal)	vosotros, vosotras (you, informal used in Spain)
usted (you, formal)	ustedes (you)
él, ella, ello (he, she, it)	ellos, ellas (they)

▶ Direct Object Pronouns

singular	plural
me (me)	nos (us)
te (you, informal)	os (you plural, informal in Spain)
lo, la (you, formal)	los, las (you plural, formal)
lo, la (him, her, it)	los, las (them)

▶ Indirect Object Pronouns

singular	plural
me (me)	nos (us)
te (you, informal)	os (you plural, informal in Spain)
le (you, formal)	les (you plural, formal)
le (him, her, it)	les (them)

singular	plural	english
mi	mis	my
tu	tus	your (familiar)
su	sus	his, her, its, your (formal)
nuestro/a	nuestros/as	our
vuestro/a	vuestros/as	your (familiar)
su	sus	their, your (formal)

▶ Reflexive Pronouns

singular	plural
me (myself)	nos (ourselves)
te (yourself, informal)	os (yourselves, informal)
se (yourself, formal)	se (yourselves, formal)
se (himself, herself, itself)	se (themselves)

Other types of pronouns might not be as easily recognizable because they don't necessarily replace a particular noun. Can you figure out which words in the following examples are pronouns?

That was a great movie.
I know who it is you like.
The calculator, which I had used on Friday, is now missing.
What was that noise?
I have everything I need.
I like them both.
They love each other.

The pronouns here are "that," "who," "which," "what," "everything," "both," and "each other." Here is how these pronouns are categorized:

Demonstrative pronouns demonstrate or point something out. In English, demonstrative pronouns are: this, that, these, and those. The word "this" in "I like this" is a good example of a demonstrative pronoun. As you can see, it replaces the thing or object which is liked.

Relative pronouns relate or connect groups of words to nouns or other pronouns. In English, relative pronouns include: "who," "whoever," "whom," "which," "that," and "whose." For example, in the phrase "I like who you like," the pronoun "who" relates "I" and "you like."

Many of the **interrogative pronouns** are identical to relative pronouns, but they are used differently—to interrogate, or ask questions. In English, interrogative pronouns include "who," "whom," "which," "whose," and "what". In the question "who do you like?" "who" is an interrogative pronoun. Note that in the answer, this pronoun will be replaced by a noun again. In Spanish, interrogative pronouns are differentiated from relative pronouns with an accent mark: quién (who?).

Indefinite pronouns are non-personal pronouns that work as nouns. There are quite a few indefinite pronouns, and many can also be used as adjectives. A few

examples in English are: "all," "none," "any," "some,"
"everyone," "someone," "no one," "much," "little,"
"few," "everything," "nothing," and "something."

Reciprocal pronouns show a mutual relationship
between two subjects. In English, there are only two
pairs of reciprocal pronouns: "each other" and "one
another." In Spanish, reflexive pronouns are used to
show reciprocity.

▶ Demonstrative Pronouns

singular	*singular*	*singular*	*plural*	*plural*	*English*
MASCULINE	FEMININE	NEUTER	MASCULINE	FEMININE	
éste	ésta	esto	éstos	éstas	this/these
ése	ésa	eso	ésos	ésas	that/those
aquél	aquélla	aquello	aquéllos	aquéllas	that/those

relative pronouns

que	that, which, who
cual(es)	which
quien(es)	who, whom, that
lo que	what, that which

▶ Indefinite Pronouns

one form

algo	something
alguien	someone
nada	nothing
nadie	no one

multiple forms

varios, varias	various
ambos, ambas	both
alguno(s), alguna(s)	some
cualquier, cualquiera(s)	whichever
mucho(s), mucha(s)	a lot
otro(s), otra(s)	other
todo(s), toda(s)	all
uno(s), una(s)	one (some)
poco(s), poca(s)	a little
ninguno(s), ninguna(s)	none

Fun and Easy Adjectives

Pronouns replace nouns, and adjectives describe or modify them. Take a look at the following phrases. Can you tell which ones are adjectives?

Siempre me contenta ver las flores bonitas.
I'm always glad to see the pretty flowers.
Un niño sano es un niño alegre.
A healthy child is a happy child.
Esa casa ha sido deshabitada por muchos años.
That house has been empty for many years.

In these examples, *bonitas* (pretty), *sano* (healthy), *alegre* (happy), *esa* (that), and *muchos* (many) are all adjectives. As you can see, in English an adjective generally comes before the noun it describes. In Spanish, the adjective generally follows the noun.

Verb: Action

At their simplest, verbs are words that signal action or being (think of it as inaction). Action verbs describe what someone or something does, whether it's in the past, present, or future:

Yo caminé hasta la casa.
I walked all the way home.
Nosotros nos hablamos a menudo.
We talk often.
Ella completará sus tareas más tarde.
She will finish her homework later.

Verbs that show a state of being are known as linking verbs: They link or show the relationship between the subject and the object:

Jenny es una estudiante.
Jenny is a student.
Aquel lugar parece hogareño.
That place looks homey.
Lo siente bien.
It feels right.

One sub-group of linking verbs are modal verbs—verbs that express mood ("can," "may," "must," "ought," "shall," "should") or verb tense (will and would). Modal verbs behave very irregularly. For example, verbs like "can" only exist in the present tense.

Adverb

It's no coincidence that the word "adverb" has the root "verb"—one of the adverb's main roles is modifying or describing the verb. Here are a few examples of adverbs:

Caminas rápido.
You walk quickly.
Te veo a menudo.
I often see you.
Lo hace cuidadosamente.
Do it carefully.

In these examples, *rápido* (quickly), *a menudo* (often), and *cuidadosamente* (carefully) are adverbs. Note that many of the adverbs in English are formed by adding the suffix "-ly" to an adjective. In Spanish, the most common adverbial suffix is *-mente*. In addition to modifying a verb, an adverb may modify an adjective or another adverb:

Lo hace muy cuidadosamente.
Do it very carefully.
Es una noche maravillosamente calma.
It's a wonderfully calm night.

In the first sentence, the adverb *muy* (very) modifies another adverb, *cuidadosamente*. In the second, *maravillosamente* (wonderfully) is an adverb that modifies the adjective *calma*, which in turn describes the noun *noche*.

In Position: Prepositions

Think of prepositions as words that signal position (physical or otherwise) of a noun or pronoun:

> Pregunta por mí.
> *Ask for me.*
> Ella está en la oficina.
> *She is at the office.*
> La caja estaba dentro de la casa.
> *The box was inside the house.*

Here, the prepositions *por* (for), *en* (at), and *dentro* (inside) explain where the noun is or how it's related to another noun (in the case of the first example). Together with the noun and article, a preposition makes up the prepositional phrases, "for me," "at the office," and "inside the house." The entire prepositional phrase functions as a complement of the verb. Without the prepositional phrase, the sentences serving as examples would not have been complete.

Conjunctions

Conjunctions and interjections play a secondary role in sentences. Conjunctions are words "at a junction"—words that join or relate words or phrases.

▶ Common Coordinating Conjunctions

o (u)	or
pero	but
sino	but
y (e)	and
a menos que	unless
a pesar de	despite
aunque	although
como	how
con todo	despite, as
cuando	when
excepto	except
más bien	rather
no obstante	in spite of, regardless
para que	so that
porque	because
que	that
salvo	except
si	if
sin embargo	nevertheless

In Agreement

Because grammar governs the role of words in a sentence, it also covers agreement (or correspondence) between words in gender, number, case, and person. In English, agreement is rarely an issue because our language doesn't rely as much on word endings to communicate information about gender (male, female, or neuter), number (singular or plural), case (role of a noun in a sentence, like whether it's a subject or an object), and person (first, second, or third). For instance, English nouns don't have gender, which means they don't have to agree in gender with articles, adjectives, or any other words. And even in plural form, adjectives and articles do not change. See the following examples.

> The red pen.
> The red pens.

In Spanish, agreement will require more of your attention. Nouns and pronouns have a particular gender (each one is either feminine or masculine) as well as number, and when paired with articles and adjectives, the endings will change accordingly:

> El coche rojo (the red car)
> Los coches rojos (the red cars)
> La manzana roja (the red apple)
> Las manzanas rojas (the red apples)

In English, the verb does not need to agree in person or number with its subject (one exception is adding -*s* to verbs in third person singular of present tense). In Spanish, the verb must be conjugated according to the person and number of its subject. See the following page for examples.

Yo camino (I walk)
Tú caminas (you walk)
José camina (José walks)
Nosotros caminamos (we walk)

Verb Conjugation

A verb is the action word in a sentence—the word that names an action (he works) or describes a state of being. Verbs are one of the most essential parts of speech, since they are a required element in sentences. Nouns, pronouns, adjectives, and so forth. don't show up in every sentence you use, but verbs do. For example, the shortest grammatically correct sentence in English is "Go!" That single word in the imperative can be a complete sentence.

Spanish verbs have to be "conjugated" or "inflected"; that is, changed according to how they are used. Each Spanish verb has at least five—but usually six—different conjugations in each tense and mood.

In most conjugations, you will need to drop the infinitive ending (leaving the radical or root) and add the appropriate ending. There are a total of five elements in conjugation: number, person, voice, mood, and tense.

Number and Person

Number and person go hand in hand; together, they indicate the grammatical person: who or what is performing the action of the verb. Number may be singular (one) or plural (more than one). Person may be first person (the speaker), second person (the listener), and third person (third party). This means there's a total of six grammatical persons, and each has at least one subject pronoun:

	singular	*plural*
1st person	yo (I)	nosotros/as (we)
2nd person	tú (you, inf.)	vosotros/as (you, inf.)
3rd person	él, ella, ello, Ud.	ellos, ellas, Uds.
	(he, she, it, you)	(they, you)

Ello is rarely used; *él* and *ella* mean "it" when they replace a noun of that gender, so *el perro* becomes *él* and *la ciudad* is replaced by *ella*. *Nosotros*, *vosotros*, and *ellos* are used for men, male nouns, and mixed gender groups. *Nosotras*, *vosotras*, and *ellas* can only be used for a group of women and/or female nouns.

In looking at the chart, you might notice what appears to be an excess of "you"s. In Spanish, two important distinctions are made when talking to "you": Is there one person or more than one? Is it someone to whom you want to indicate closeness (a friend, parent, pet) or someone to whom you wish to show respect (a doctor, teacher, lawyer)? Once you've answered these questions, you'll know which "you" to use: In Spain, *tú* is singular/informal, *Ud.* is singular/formal, *vosotros* (vosotras in the feminine) is plural/informal, and *Uds.* is plural/formal. In Latin America, *vosotros* is no longer in use; instead, *Uds.* is used for all plural "you"s.

Making Sense of Tense

Tense refers to the time a verb's action takes place: present, past, or future. A **simple tense** is a verb form that consists of a single word like *hablamos* (we talk). A **compound tense** is a verb form made up of two words: auxiliary verb + participle: *he comido* (I have eaten), *estamos hablando* (we are talking). Note that *escucharé* is a simple tense in Spanish, while its translation "will listen" is a compound tense in English.

Get in the Mood

Mood refers to the attitude of the speaker toward the action/state of the verb—how likely or factual the statement is. Spanish has three moods: indicative, subjunctive, and imperative. The indicative is what you might call the "normal" mood—it indicates a fact: *Vivimos en España.* (We live in Spain.)

The subjunctive expresses subjectivity, such as doubt and unlikelihood: *Quiero que lo hagas.* (I want you to do it.) Note that the subjunctive is extremely rare in English but common in Spanish. The imperative is the mood of command: *Esperad aquí.* (Wait here.)

Verb Forms

Once you know the tense and mood that you would like to use, you have a verb form and you can start figuring out its conjugations. There are more than two dozen Spanish verb forms, the most important of which will be explained in this chapter.

Four Types of Verbs

There are four main types of Spanish verbs: regular, stem-changing, irregular, and reflexive. Most Spanish verbs are regular, which means they are conjugated according to a pattern. Once you learn how to conjugate one regular –AR, –ER, and –IR verb, you can conjugate the majority of Spanish verbs.

Regular Verbs

To conjugate regular verbs in the present tense, all you need to do is drop the infinitive ending of the verb, and choose the correct ending based on the verb's group (whether it's an –AR, –ER, or –IR verb), person, and number.

–AR Verbs		–ER Verbs		–IR Verbs	
–o	–amos	–o	–emos	–o	–imos
–as	–áis	–es	–éis	–es	–ís
–a	–an	–e	–en	–e	–en

As examples, let's take the verbs *hablar* (to speak), *vender* (to sell), and *vivir* (to live):

(yo) hablo, vendo, vivo
(nosotros, nosotras) hablamos, vendemos, vivimos
(tú) hablas, vendes, vives
(vosotros, vosotras) habláis, vendéis, vivís
(él, ella, usted) habla, vende, vive
(ellos, ellas) hablan, venden, viven

Hablo alemán.
I speak German.
¿Vivís aquí?
Do you live here?

Stem-Changing Verbs

Stem-changing verbs are verbs that undergo a change in the root (radical) in various conjugations. The three stem changes are E > IE, O > UE, and E > I.

The following examples show how the stem is changed in the present indicative of *querer*, *poder*, and *pedir*.

querer (to want)

yo quiero	*nosotros queremos*
tú quieres	*vosotros queréis*
él quiere	*ellos quieren*

poder (can, to be able to)

yo puedo	*nosotros podemos*
tú puedes	*vosotros podéis*
él puede	*ellos pueden*

repetir (to repeat)

yo repito	*nosotros repetimos*
tú repites	*vosotros repetís*
él repite	*ellos repiten*

Spelling-Change Verbs

Aside from stem-changing verbs, which are characterized by changes in vowels, there are certain Spanish verbs that undergo consonant spelling changes in certain conjugations. The consonants that are generally affected are C, G, and, to a lesser extent, Z. Before E and I, C sounds like S and G sounds like a hard H (or Spanish J). The letter Z cannot precede E or I; that means it must be replaced by the letter C.

When conjugating verbs, the sound of the last letter before the ending (e.g., the C in *sacar*, the G in *jugar*) needs to be maintained in every tense and mood. As a result, some verbs require a spelling modification.

For example, the verb *pagar* (to pay) has a hard G sound, which is maintained with all of the present tense conjugations because they are all hard vowels (*pago, pagas, paga*, etc.). However in the preterite, the first person singular ends in the soft vowel E, which would normally give you "*pagé*" and would be pronounced [*pa hay*]. What you want is [*pa gay*], so to get that sound you need to change the spelling to *pagué*.

Reflections on Reflexive Verbs

Reflexive verbs are classified according to their regular/irregular/stem-changing verb classification, but have an additional characteristic: they are preceded by a reflexive pronoun, which indicates that the subject is performing the action of the verb upon itself (*me lavo*, I'm washing myself) or that multiple subjects are performing a reciprocal action (*se escriben*, they write to each other). Many verbs have both reflexive and nonreflexive uses. For example, *escribir* means "to write" (a letter, a book, etc.), whereas *escribirse* means "to write to each other."

When you are conjugating a reflexive verb, each grammatical person must be matched with a reflexive pronoun:

lavarse (to wash oneself)

yo me lavo	*nosotros nos lavamos*
tú te lavas	*vosotros os laváis*
él se lava	*ellos se lavan*

Indirect Object Pronoun Verbs

There is another category of verbs that includes *gustarle* (to like) and *faltarle* (to need, be lacking). These verbs are unusual for two reasons: They require an indirect object pronoun (indicated by *le* tacked on to the infinitive) and they do not conjugate according to grammatical person, but rather according to the number of the noun that follows.

Take the phrase "I like school" as an example. "School" is singular, so the verb, *gustar*, will be in the third person singular, and we end up with *me gusta la escuela*. In the sentence, "I like books," the subject "books" is plural, so the verb will be conjugated in the third person plural: *me gustan los libros*.

me gusta el libro	nos gusta el libro
me gustan los libros	nos gustan los libros
te gusta el libro	os gusta el libro
te gustan los libros	os gustan los libros
le gusta el libro	les gusta el libro
le gustan los libros	les gustan los libros

Present Tense

The present tense (*el presente*) of the indicative mood is very similar in usage to the English present tense. The one difference is that in Spanish, "I eat" and "I am eating" are both translated as (*yo*) *como*. If you want to emphasize the fact that you are eating right now, you can use the Spanish present progressive, *yo estoy comiendo*, covered later in the chapter.

In the present tense, regular verbs are conjugated by dropping the infinitive ending and adding the following endings:

–AR Verbs		–ER Verbs		–IR Verbs	
–o	–amos	–o	–emos	–o	–imos
–as	–áis	–es	–éis	–es	–ís
–a	–an	–e	–en	–e	–en

Simple Past (Preterite)

The preterite (*el pretérito*) is the Spanish simple past tense, used to talk about specific actions or events that were completed in the past. In the preterite, most regular Spanish verbs are conjugated with the radical (verb minus infinitive ending) plus the appropriate preterite ending.

–AR Verbs		–ER and –IR Verbs		Irregular Verb Endings	
–é	–amos	–í	–imos	–e	–imos
–aste	–asteis	–iste	–isteis	–iste	–isteis
–ó	–aron	–ió	–ieron	–o	–ieron

Stem-changing verbs that end in –AR or –ER do not stem-change in the preterite; stem-changing –IR verbs do go through a stem change in the third person conjugations: those that have an E change to an I, and those that have an O change to a U.

Some verbs are irregular in the preterite; you'll need to memorize their radicals and use them with the irregular set of endings (listed in the preceding table). These verbs are *estar* (to be), *poder* (to be able to), *poner* (to put), *querer* (to want), *tener* (to have), and *venir* (to come).

Other verbs that are irregular in the preterite include *dar* (to give), *ver* (to see), *decir* (to say), *traer* (to bring), *hacer* (to do), *ser* (to be), and *ir* (to go).

The Imperfect Tense

The imperfect tense (*el imperfecto*) is used to talk about a past action or state of being without specifying when it began or ended. It is often equivalent to the construction "was/were . . . –ing" in English. The Spanish imperfect is also used for descriptions, like *hacía calor* (it was hot) and can express repeated actions in the past, such as *llamaba todos los días* (I used to call every day).

Except for *ir*, *ser*, and *ver*, all Spanish verbs have regular conjugations in this tense, formed with the following endings:

−AR Verbs	−ER Verbs	−IR Verbs	
−aba	−ábamos	−ía	−íamos
−abas	−abais	−ías	−íais
−aba	−aban	−ía	−ían

Future and Conditional

Future and conditional tenses are both formed with the entire infinitive form (without dropping the −AR, −ER, or −IR ending) plus the appropriate ending. A handful of verbs have irregular future/conditional radicals, but they use the same endings as regular verbs:

Verb	Radical	Verb	Radical
caber	cabr−	querer	querr−
decir	dir−	reír	reir−
haber	habr−	saber	sabr−
hacer	har−	salir	saldr−
oír	oir−	tener	tendr−
poder	podr−	valer	valdr−
poner	pondr−	venir	vendr−

The Spanish future tense (*el futuro*) is used much like its English counterpart ("will" + verb)— to announce upcoming events. The conditional (*el potencial*) is used for actions that are not guaranteed to occur; often they are dependent on certain conditions. In English, this verb form is indicated by the word "would."

Future Endings for All Verbs

–é	–emos
–ás	–éis
–á	–án

Conditional Endings for All Verbs

–ía	–íamos
–ías	–íais
–ía	–ían

For example, *yo hablaré* (I'll speak), *ella venderá* (she'll sell), *nosotros viviremos* (we'll live), *ellos tendrán* (they'll have); *yo hablaría* (I'd speak), *ella vendería* (she'd sell), *nosotros viviríamos* (we'd live), *ellos tendrían* (they'd have).

In the Mood to Command

The imperative (*el imperativo*) is a verb mood used to give a command, either affirmative (Go!) or negative (Don't go!). The imperative for all commands for *Ud., Uds.,* and *nosotros* and for negative commands for *tú* and *vosotros* is formed by taking the present indicative form and then changing one letter:

- **Regular –AR verbs:** Change the A at the beginning of the ending to E.
- **Regular –ER verbs:** Change the E at the beginning of the ending to A.
- **Regular –IR verbs:** In the *tú, Ud.,* and *Uds.* forms, change the E at the beginning of the ending to A. In the *nosotros* form, change the I of the ending to A. In the *vosotros* form, change the Í of the ending to ÁI. (Note that the imperative endings for –ER and –IR verbs end up being identical.)

–AR Verbs in the Imperative

present indicative	positive command	negative command
tú estudias	estudia	no estudies
Ud. estudia	estudie	no estudie
nosotros estudiamos	estudiemos	no estudiemos
vosotros estudiáis	estudiad	no estudiéis
Uds. estudian	estudien	no estudien

–ER Verbs in the Imperative

present indicative	positive command	negative command
tú bebes	bebe	no bebas
Ud. bebe	beba	no beba
nosotros bebemos	bebamos	no bebamos
vosotros bebéis	bebed	no bebáis
Uds. beben	beban	no beban

–IR Verbs in the Imperative

present indicative	positive command	negative command
tú abres	abre	no abras
Ud. abre	abra	no abra
nosotros abrimos	abramos	no abramos
vosotros abrís	abrid	no abráis
Uds. abren	abran	no abran

The Subjunctive Mood

The subjunctive mood (*el subjuntivo*) is subjective; it expresses emotional, potential, and hypothetical attitudes about what is being expressed—things like will/wanting, emotion, doubt, possibility, necessity, and judgment. Subjunctive conjugations are similar to imperative conjugations, in the sense that the endings "switch": –AR verbs take on E endings, and –ER and –IR verbs take on A endings.

–AR Verbs	–ER Verbs	–IR Verbs	
–e	–emos	–a	–amos
–es	–éis	–as	–áis
–e	–en	–a	–an

Stem-changing verbs use the same endings for subjunctive conjugations as regular verbs but may undergo spelling changes. Stem-changing –AR and –ER verbs follow the rules for regular verbs: they use the same stem as in the present tense and thus maintain their stem changes in the subjunctive.

However, stem-changing –IR verbs are irregular in the subjunctive.

Most verbs that have an irregular first person singular (*yo*) *conjugation* in the present indicative tense use that conjugation as the basis for their subjunctive stem. For example: *conocer > conozco > conozca*.

Some verbs have an irregular subjunctive stem that must be memorized: *haber* (perfect auxiliary verb), *ir* (to go), *saber* (to know), and *ser* (to be). The following verb groups change the final letter in the stem due to the issue of hard/soft vowels:

- Verbs that end in –*car* (C > QU).
- Verbs that end in –*gar* (G > GU).
- Verbs that end in –*zar* (Z > C).

Imperfect Subjunctive

The imperfect tense of the subjunctive mood (*el imperfecto de subjuntivo*) is used to express the same subjectivity as the present subjunctive, but in the past. It is most commonly found in unlikely *si* (if) clauses: *Si tuviera dinero, iría.* (If I had money, I would go.)

To conjugate the imperfect subjunctive for any verb, take the third person plural preterite form, drop the –*ron* ending to find the radical, and add the appropriate endings (choosing from either the –*ra* or the –*se* group). See the examples on the following page.

−ra Conjugations		−se Conjugations	
−ra	− ́ramos	−se	− ́semos
−ras	−rais	−ses	−seis
−ra	−ran	−se	−sen

Progressive Tenses and Moods

The progressive tenses indicate something in progress—the equivalent of "to be + –ing" in English. The progressive tenses are conjugated with *estar* as the auxiliary verb plus the present participle. For example, present progressive uses the present form of *estar*: *estoy estudiando* (I am studying).

The present participle in English is the "–ing" form of the verb (also known as a gerund). In Spanish, it's the *–ndo* form. The formation of the Spanish present participle is fairly easy.

> **Regular –AR verbs:** Drop the infinitive ending and add *–ando*; *hablar—hablando*.
> **Regular –ER and –IR verbs:** Drop the infinitive ending and add *–iendo*; *aprender—aprendiendo, escribir—escribiendo*.
> **Verbs with stems that end in vowel:** Drop the infinitive and add *–yendo*; *leer—leyendo*.
> **–IR verbs with stem-change in third-person preterite form keep that stem change:** *decir—diciendo*.
> **Ir (to go) has an irregular gerund:** *yendo*.

Perfect Tenses and Moods

The perfect tenses use *haber* as the auxiliary verb plus the past participle. Note that "perfect" here does not mean flawless, but rather completed, indicating that perfect tenses and moods are those which describe a completed action at some point in time and possibility.

Perfect Tenses

tense	example in yo form
present perfect	*he comido* (I have eaten)
past perfect	*había comido* (I had eaten)
future perfect	*habré comido* (I will have eaten)
conditional perfect	*habría comido* (I would have eaten)
past subjunctive	*que haya comido* (that I have eaten)
pluperfect subjunctive	*que hubiera comido* (that I had eaten)

Forming past participles isn't difficult:

Regular –AR verbs: Drop the infinitive ending and add *–ado*; *hablar—hablado*.

Regular –ER and –IR verbs: Drop the infinitive ending and add *–ido*; *aprender—aprendido, venir—venido*.

Verbs with radical that ends in vowel: Drop the infinitive and add *–ído*; *leer—leído*.

A few past participles are simply irregular and will have to be memorized. See the verb charts in Appendix C for more.

04 / Pronunciation and Writing

PART OF LEARNING a language is being able to write in it. This means being able to spell correctly, knowing the rules of capitalization and punctuation, and knowing how to proofread your work—dotting the i's and crossing the t's, so to speak.

Don't Overcapitalize

Overall, the rules of capitalization are very similar in English and in Spanish. Capitalization is used in three basic ways:

1. To indicate the beginning of a sentence.
2. To distinguish proper names.
3. In titles of books, movies, lectures, and so on; in headers.

The first rule should be pretty clear. Be sure to capitalize the first word of every new sentence, just as you do in English.

The second rule, which deals with proper names, is also pretty similar in English and in Spanish. Names of people, cities, and countries are capitalized in both languages:

Me llamo Benicio Juan Armandez.
My name is Benicio Juan Armandez.
Vivo en Buenos Aires, la capital de Argentina.
I live in Buenos Aires, the capital of Argentina.

Brand names are also considered proper names:

Prefiero las zapatillas de deportes marca Nike.
I prefer Nike sneakers.

However, the third rule of capitalization isn't exactly identical in English and Spanish. In English, we generally capitalize most of the words in a title or header (the exceptions being prepositions shorter than six letters and articles, although these rules may vary). In Spanish, only the first word of the header or title is capitalized:

El autor de la novela Cien años de soledad es Gabriel García Márquez.
The author of the novel A Hundred Years of Solitude is Gabriel García Márquez.

¿Has visto la película Tráfico?
Have you seen the movie Traffic?

This pretty much takes care of capitalization in Spanish. Although we have additional capitalization rules in English, none of them apply in Spanish.

Days of the week: In Spanish, the days of the week are written in lowercase letters: *lunes, martes, miércoles, jueves, viernes, sábado, domingo* (Monday, Tuesday, and so on).

Months of the year: The same is true of the twelve months of the year: *enero, febrero, marzo, abril, mayo, junio, julio, agosto, septiembre, octubre, noviembre, diciembre* (January, February, and so on).

Languages and Nationality: It is unnecessary to capitalize languages and nationalities:

> Yo soy rusa. Hablo ruso, inglés y castellano.
> *I am Russian. I speak Russian, English, and Spanish.*
> ¿Se habla francés en Canadá?
> *Is French spoken in Canada?*

Religious Denominations: Finally, don't worry about capitalizing names of religions:

> Soy judía; mi religión es judaísmo.
> *I am Jewish; my religion is Judaism.*
> La religión más común entre los latinos es el catolicismo.
> *The most common religion among Latinos is Catholicism.*

The Rules of Punctuation

As with capitalization, the general rules of punctuation in Spanish are not very different from the rules in English. The punctuation signs in use are pretty much the same:

- *El punto* (period) is used to mark the end of the sentence.
- *La coma* (comma) has a variety of uses, such as separating a series of like terms, except when the comma precedes the conjunctions *y*, *e*, *o*, and *u*
- *Dos puntos* (colon) is used to introduce a point or a series of terms.
- *Punto y coma* (semicolon) is used to separate independent clauses.
- *El guión* (dash, hyphen) has the same applications in English and in Spanish, but it has an additional use in Spanish.
- *Los signos de interrogación* (question marks) are used to indicate questions. The difference is that you need two question marks to enclose the question.
- *Los signos de exclamación* (exclamation marks) are used to indicate exclamations. You need two exclamation marks to enclose the exclamation.
- **Comillas** (quotation marks) are used in Spanish only in the case of highlighting a word, phrase, or a quote; they're not used to indicate dialogue.

The major difference between English and Spanish pronunciation is punctuating words of dialogue. Instead of quotation marks, a dash is used in Spanish to indicate the start of dialogue. Furthermore, there's no rule that each speaker's words are separated by a hard return. Take a look at the following example:

> Estoy tan cansado— dijo Ramón. —Vamos a descansar por un
>   rato— respondió Elena.
> *"I am so tired," said Ramon.*
> *"Let's rest a while," responded Elena.*

Another difference is that commas and periods are placed outside of quotation marks, unless these punctuation marks are a part of the original quote: . . . "*ejemplo*", . . . "*ejemplo*".

The final difference is the use of the comma and period in decimals and numerals with more than three digits. In Spanish, the usage is inverted so that decimal points are separated with a comma and numerals with more than three digits are separated by periods:

> Two thousand = 2.000
> Two and a quarter = 2,25

When in Doubt—Look It Up

If you plan to write on your PC or Mac, there's good news—you can probably switch your language option to Spanish and your word processing program may even provide you with a spell checker and a grammar checker. Even if it's not installed on your computer, you can probably download good software online.

The extra effort is definitely worth it. The software can help you catch mistakes so that next time you'll do it right the first time. However, don't forget that no program is perfect—it's meant to be a good resource, but you shouldn't accept all the corrections without question. As in English, you still have to make decisions about what is right and what is wrong. A spell checker will not catch you misusing a Spanish word— it can only catch misspellings. Similarly, a grammar checker may point out a commonly misused grammatical construction that you used correctly. Trust yourself to know which mistakes are really mistakes.

When you are in doubt, double-check yourself. In addition to this book, there are many other resources you can rely on. If you feel uncomfortable with verb conjugations, invest in *The Everything® Spanish Verb Book*. And make sure you have a good Spanish to English/English to Spanish dictionary with detailed entries, like *The Oxford Spanish Dictionary* or the *Larousse Standard Dictionary: Spanish-English/ English-Spanish*.

You can also take advantage of online resources. *Wordreference.com* provides online dictionaries for Spanish, English, and a host of other languages. Verb conjugation help is also available online, but be sure that you're using a reputable Web site that is not full of mistakes and misinformation.

Accent Marks, Ñ, and Other Symbols

If you can switch to Spanish in your word processing software, it may auto-correct you when you type by adding the right Spanish symbols as appropriate—the accent marks over vowels, the tilde (that squiggly mark over the soft "n"), and even upside-down question marks and exclamation marks (¿ and ¡). Test it out. For questions and exclamations, try starting with a regular question mark or exclamation mark—the symbol should flip upside-down automatically.

If you don't have Spanish as a language option, or if your paper is mostly in English but requires the use of Spanish passages, you'll need to learn the shortcuts for inserting the right symbols and accents as you type.

On a PC

One way to insert accent marks, ñ, ¿, and ¡ is by using the Symbol menu usually found on the toolbar under the Tools category. Scroll down to find the right symbol, click on it, and press Insert. You'll see it appear in the document.

Another option is to use a series of shortcut key strokes. To add an accent mark, first press down and release two keys: Control + ' (apostrophe). Then type in the vowel that you wish to accent: a, e, i, o, or u. To key in ñ, press down Control + ~ (this is actually three keys, since ~ is a combination of Shift + `). Release and type "n." If á, é, í, ó, ú, or ñ are capital letters, use Shift when you type a, e, i, o, u, or n.

To add an upside-down question mark, use the following key strokes: Shift + Control + Alt + ? If you need an upside-down exclamation mark, type in Shift + Control + Alt + ! If you don't like these shortcuts, you may be able to make your own. Go back to that Symbol window and poke around.

On a Mac

If you're using the Mac version of Microsoft Word, the Symbol menu is pretty much identical—just look under Tools. But if you'd like to use the shortcut key strokes, they're slightly different.

To add an accent mark to a vowel, hold down Option + e; release, then type in the vowel that needs the accent—a, e, i, o, or u. Again, if the accented vowel is a capital letter, add the Shift key to the second step. To insert "ñ," simply type in Option + n (or Option + Shift + n to get Ñ).

And adding ¿ and ¡ is even easier. To get the upside-down question mark, type in Option + ? For the upside-down exclamation mark, use Option + 1.

Composing a Letter

Overall, writing in Spanish isn't very different. You can use the same formats you've always relied on when composing poems, short stories, essays, and other forms of writing. None of these forms is very rigid in their structure and there aren't really any conventions you need to be aware of.

The one exception to this rule is letter-writing. Learning how to compose formal and informal letters will come in handy if you'd like to have a Spanish-speaking pen-pal, if you're planning to study or work abroad, or if your business has international branches and you need to communicate with them.

Formal Letters

Begin your letter by writing the place (where you are) and date in the top right-hand corner. You can use the following format:

Nueva York, 2 de enero de 2005

Next, include the "dear ____" line. If you know the person you're writing to, you can simply use *Señor* (or *Señora/Señores/Señoras*); another option is to add *estimado* (esteemed):

Estimado Señor
Estimadas Señoras

If the addressee is unknown, you can write *A quien corresponda* (to whom it may concern). The biggest difference here is that there's no punctuation (comma or colon) at the end of this line.

Insert an extra space and continue with the body of the letter. There are no rules here. Write down what needs to be communicated and don't forget to be polite and use the *usted/ustedes* form of address. To close the letter, choose any of the following formal closings:

Atentamente	*Sincerely*
Atentos saludos de	*Sincere greetings from*
Un cordial saludo	*A cordial greeting*

Again, there's no punctuation following the closing. Simply sign your name underneath. If you need to add a post scriptum (P.S.) line, it should be labeled P.D. (post data).

Informal Letters

If your letter is informal, there are things you would do differently. One common way of addressing your reader or readers is with the adjective *querido* (dear):

Querida Ana	*Dear Ana*
Querido hermano	*Dear brother*
Queridos amigos	*Dear friends*

In closing, appropriate sign-offs include:

Un abrazo de	*With a hug*
Un cariñoso saludo	*An affectionate greeting*
Tu amiga	*Your friend*

05 / Putting It Together

I Have a Question

Asking questions in Spanish isn't very different from how we do it in English—but you probably never even thought about how it's done in English and did it automatically. Now you'll have to pay attention. To form a question in Spanish, there are four basic options:

1. Raising your voice at the end of the sentence.
2. Inverting the subject and verb.
3. Adding a question phrase at the end of the statement.
4. Using a question word.

The first option is simplest. As you ask the following question, your voice should rise by the time you get to "ña" in *mañana*:

¿El electricista llega mañana?
The electrician will come tomorrow?

To emphasize what you're asking, you can also invert the subject and verb of the sentence. In this example, the subject *tú* and the verb *eres* switch places:

¿Eres tú la actriz del teatro Colón en Argentina?
Are you the actress from the Colon theater in Argentina?

It's also possible to turn a statement into a question by adding a question word or phrase to the end of it:

Están de acuerdo conmigo, ¿verdad?
You agree with me, right?
Hoy es miércoles, ¿no es así?
Today is Wednesday, isn't it?

Other question words and phrases that may be added to the end of statements include the following:

¿no es cierto?	isn't it certain?
¿no?	or not?
¿sí?	right?
¿eh?	huh? (waiting for confirmation)

You can ask questions by using question words like ¿*qué*? (what?), ¿*cómo*? (how?), ¿*cuándo*? (when?), ¿*dónde*? (where?), ¿*cuál*? (which), and ¿*quién*? (who?).

¿Dónde está la florería?
Where is the florist's shop located?

¿Quién es la chica con los pantalones blancos?
Who is the girl in white pants?

Yes, No, or Maybe

For the first three groups of questions, the expected answer may be *sí* (yes), *no* (no), or any of the words we might translate as "maybe": *quizá* (or *quizás*), *tal vez*, and *a lo mejor*. Another way of saying "maybe" is with a verb phrase—*puede que* or *puede ser que*. Note that the clause the follows will be in the subjunctive mood.

Let's look at some examples of questions and answers. Let's say the question is:

¿Es Londres la capital de Inglaterra?
Is London the capital of England?

Here are some appropriate responses:

Sí, Londres es la capital de Inglaterra.
Yes, London is the capital of England.
No, Londres no es la capital de Inglaterra. Es la capital del Reino
　　Unido.
*No, London isn't the capital of England. It's the capital of the
　　United Kingdom.*
Tal vez Londres es la capital de Inglaterra, no estoy seguro.
Maybe London is the capital of England, I'm not sure.
Puede ser que Londres sea la capital de Inglaterra.
Maybe (it's possible) that London is the capital of England.

Question Words

Journalists are taught that to write a good story, they must answer the five W questions: who, what, where, when, and why. Let's get acquainted with the Spanish question words (also known as interrogatives) that are the equivalent of these, plus a few others.

Qué—What's Going On?

To ask "what?" use the question word *¿qué?*

¿Qué es esto?
What is this?
¿Qué tipo de corte de pelo prefieres?
What type of haircut do you prefer?

¿Qué? may be used in conjunction with a preposition:

¿con qué?	how? with what?
¿de qué?	of what? from what?
¿para qué?	why? for what purpose?
¿por qué?	why?

In Spanish there's no separate word for "why?" You can use either *¿para qué?* or *¿por qué?* The first of the two is used to ask "for what purpose?" while the second is a more traditional form of "why?" Compare:

¿Para qué estás aquí?
Why are you here? (For what purpose are you here?)

¿Por qué estás aquí?
Why are you here? (What's the reason?)

Quién—Look Who's Talking

There are two forms of the question "who?" in Spanish: *¿quién?* (singular) and *¿quiénes?* (plural):

¿Quién es el presidente de los Estados Unidos?
Who is the president of the United States?
¿Quiénes son los líderes del equipo?
Who are the team leaders?

Other question words based on *¿quién?* and *¿quiénes?* are:

¿a quién?	whom? (singular)
¿a quiénes?	whom? (plural)
¿con quién?	with whom? (singular)
¿con quiénes?	with whom? (plural)
¿de quién?	whose? (singular)
¿de quiénes?	whose? (plural)

¿A quién debo contactar para conseguir la información?
Whom should I contact to get the information?
¿De quiénes son estos libros?
Whose books are these?

Dónde—Where It's At

The question "where?" is *¿dónde?* in Spanish. This question word is used to ask about location of a person or thing and is often used with the verb *estar* (to be):

¿Dónde están los zapatos rojos de tacón alto?
Where are the red high-heeled shoes?

When the verb of the question is a verb of motion, like *ir* (to go) or *caminar* (to walk), use the question word *¿adónde?* (to where?):

¿Adónde van los chicos?
Where are the boys going?
¿Adónde camina aquella gente?
Where are those people walking?

In adónde, the *a* represents "to," so the questions in the last examples are really "To where are the boys going?" and "To where are those people walking?" Other question phrases that may be formed with *dónde* are:

¿de dónde?	from where?
¿hacia dónde?	toward where?
¿para dónde?	toward where?

Cuánto—How Much and How Many

In English, there are two question phrases that may be used when asking about quantity. If you're asking about quantifiable things (things that you can count, like apples or chairs or doctors), the right question is "how many?" If you're asking about unquantifiable things (water, money, time), you'll ask "how much?"

In Spanish, both questions are translated as variants of *¿cuánto?* If you mean "how many?" the question word is plural and must agree with the gender of the objects being counted. That means you've got two options: *¿cuántos?* and *¿cuántas?* If the question is "how much," the question word has to be in its singular form, so the two options are *¿cuánto?* and *¿cuánta?*

Here are a few examples:

> ¿Cuánto tiempo tienes para mí?
> *How much time do you have for me?*
> ¿Cuántos amigos te visitaron?
> *How many friends visited you?*

In the previous examples, the question word *cuánto* was used as an adjective—it modified *tiempo*, *energía*, *amigos*, and *muñecas*. But *cuánto* can also be used on its own as a pronoun:

> ¿Cuánto cuestan los tomates?
> *How much are the tomatoes?*

In this case, *cuánto* is not the adjective of *dinero* (money)—instead, it replaces it.

Cuál—Which Is It, Anyway?

"Which?" in Spanish has two versions, a singular and a plural: *¿cuál?* and *¿cuáles?* However, *cuál/cuáles* and "which" aren't necessarily equivalent. When "which?" is used as an adjective before a noun, the correct translation is *¿qué?*

¿Qué tipo de tela prefieres?
Which kind of fabric do you prefer?
¿Qué frutas te gusta comer?
Which fruit do you like to eat?

On the other hand, sometimes *cuál/cuáles* is needed when a good English translation calls for "what?"

¿Cuál es la fecha de hoy?
What (which) day is it today?
¿Cuál es la capital de Perú?
What is the capital of Peru?

Cómo and Cuándo—How and When

The last two question words are relatively simple—both *¿cómo?* and *¿cuándo?* have a direct equivalent in English: "how" and "when," respectively.

¿Cómo se dice "Irlanda" en inglés?
How do you say Irlanda in English?
¿Cuándo regresará mamá?
When will mom come back?

Practice Makes Perfect

Now that we've reviewed the basic question formats and the question words, let's end with a review of frequently asked questions.

¿Cómo te llamas? ¿Cómo se llama?
What's your name? (informal and formal)
¿Cuál es la fecha de hoy?
What day is it today?
¿Cuánto cuesta el pan? ¿Cuánto cuestan las piñas?
How much is the bread? How much are the pineapples?
¿Cúantos años tienes? ¿Cuántos años tiene usted?
How old are you? (informal and formal)
¿Qué significa esto?
What does this mean?
¿Me entiendes? ¿Me entiende?
Do you understand me? (informal and formal)

If you didn't understand the answer, you can say *¿Cómo?* (What?) to clarify.

06 / Useful Words and Phrases

In Flight

You've got a long flight ahead of you. What better time to try out your language skills? Start up a conversation with the Spanish-speaker in the seat next to you, or chat with the bilingual flight attendant. If you're traveling on a foreign airline, Spanish may very well come in handy if you need to ask a member of the flight crew a question.

Refer back to Chapter 5 for a refresher on forming questions in Spanish.

Why has the plane been delayed?
¿Por qué el avión está retrasado?
My seatbelt won't fasten.
Mi cinturón no abrocha.
May I have a blanket?
¿Puedo tener una manta?
I'd like a vegetarian meal.
Quisiera una comida vegetariana.

What time are we going to land?
¿A qué hora vamos a aterrizar?
May I change my seat?
¿Puedo cambiar mi asiento?
I'd like an aisle seat.
Quisiera un asiento junto al pasillo.
I'd like a window seat.
Quisiera un asiento junto a la ventana.
What movie are we going to see?
¿Cuál película vamos a ver?
May I have some water?
¿Puedo tener un poco de agua?

▶ **In-Flight Vocabulary**

emergency exit	la salida de emergencia
life vest	el chaleco salvavidas
airplane	el avión
pilot	el piloto, la pilota
altitude	la altitud
baggage	el portaequipajes
row	la fila
seat	el asiento
pillow	la almohada
take-off	el despegue
landing	el aterrizaje
headphones	los auriculares
flight attendant	el/la azafato/a
boarding card	el pase de abordar
carry-on luggage	equipaje de mano

Navigating the Airport

You've arrived! Now let's get you through the airport, past customs, and on your way.

▶ Airport Vocabulary

arrival	la llegada
baggage	el equipaje
baggage claim	reclamación de equipajes
boarding gate	la puerta de embarque
bus stop	la parada de autobús
car rental	el alquiler de coches
cart	el carrito
departure	la salida
elevator	los ascensores
entrance	la entrada
exit	la salida
flight	el vuelo
to miss the flight	perder el vuelo
money exchange	el cambio de dinero
lost baggage	el equipaje extraviado
lost and found	la oficina de objetos perdidos
moving walkway	las cintas transportadoras
restrooms	los baños
ticket	el boleto
hallway	el pasillo

Declaring Your Belongings

The verb *tener*, "to have" will come in handy as you pass through customs. Use it to express what you have or don't have with you.

TENER: to have	
yo tengo	*nosotros tenemos*
tú tienes	*vosotros tenéis*
él, ella, usted tiene	*ellos, ellas, ustedes tienen*

Tener is used in Spanish in the same way we use the verb "to have" in English:

Tengo dos hijos.
I have two children.
Carla tiene una visa estudiantil.
Clara has a student visa.
Tenemos familia aquí.
We have family here.

Just as in English, the verb *tener* can be used in the expression "to have to (do something)." In Spanish, the phrase is *tener que* + infinitive:

Tengo que salir ahora.
I have to leave now.
Tienen que sentarse juntos.
They have to sit together.

▶ Customs Vocabulary

customs	la aduana
duty free	libre de impuestos
flight number	el número de vuelo
form of identification	la forma de identificación
passport	el pasaporte

In addition to the vocabulary, here are some questions and phrases for going through the customs:

Here is my passport.
Aquí está mi pasaporte.
Do you have anything to declare?
¿Tiene algo que declarar?
Yes, I have something to declare.
Sí, tengo algo que declarar.
I have nothing to declare.
No tengo nada que declarar.
I'm here on business.
Estoy aquí de negocios.
I'm here on vacation.
Estoy aquí de vacaciones.
I'll be here for two weeks.
Estaré aquí dos semanas.
I'm going to stay at the Hotel Gran Vía.
Me voy a quedar en el Hotel Gran Vía.

Staying at a Hotel

You've made it from the airport to the hotel front desk. And you've been using your Spanish all the way, thanks to this book, haven't you? Now, let's get you checked in. Courtesy is extremely important in many Spanish-speaking cultures. Remember to say *por favor* (please) and *gracias* (thank you), and you'll get much better service. And as always, when in doubt, use the formal you, *usted*.

I have a reservation.
Tengo una reservación.
I don't have a reservation.
No tengo reservación.
I'll be staying for three nights.
Me voy a quedar tres noches.
We'd like a double bed.
Quisiéramos una cama matrimonial.
We'd like a room with a private bath.
Quisiéramos un cuarto con baño privado.
Please give me a wake-up call at 7 a.m.
Por favor, llame para despertarme a las siete de la mañana.
How do you make an outside call?
¿Cómo se marca para la calle?
Our room hasn't been cleaned.
No han limpiado nuestro cuarto.
The bill is incorrect.
La cuenta no está correcta.

I'm ready to check out.
Estoy listo/a para desocupar.
Can I have the bill, please?
¿Puedo tener la cuenta, por favor?

▶ Hotel Vocabulary

air-conditioning	el aire acondicionado
bar	el bar
bathroom	el cuarto de baño
bathtub	la bañera
bed	la cama
double bed	la cama matrimonial
twin bed	la cama individual
bill	la cuenta
doorman	el portero
elevator	el ascensor
floor	el piso
gym	el gimnasio
hairdryer	el secador de pelo
hanger	la percha
hostel	el hostal
hotel	el hotel
ice cubes	los cubitos de hielo
key	la llave
lamp	la lámpara
light	la luz
manager	el/la gerente
pillow	la almohada
reservation	la reservación

▶ **Hotel Vocabulary** *(continued)*

room	la habitación
safe (box)	la caja de seguridad
shampoo	el champú
sheet	la sábana
shower	la ducha
swimming pool	la piscina
telephone	el teléfono
television	la televisión
toilet	el water, el inodoro
toilet paper	el papel higiénico
towel	la toalla
bath towel	la toalla de baño
face towel	la toalla para la cara
hand towel	la toalla para las manos
sink	el lavabo
water	el agua
cold water	el agua fría
hot water	el agua caliente
window	la ventana

Running Errands

After a delicious lunch in Oaxaca, you realize more mole landed on your suit than in your mouth. You catch your reflection in the pond in *el Parque Retiro* in Madrid and notice that it's been way too long since your last haircut. Climbing into a *chivo* in Cartagena, your boot heel catches on the stair and snaps right off. You need some professional help.

What time do you open?
¿A qué hora abre usted?
What time do you close?
¿A qué hora cierra usted?
Are you open on Sundays?
¿Está abierto los domingos?
Can you help me, please?
¿Puede usted ayudarme, por favor?
How much do I owe you?
¿Cuánto le debo?
Can I pay with a credit card?
¿Puedo pagar con tarjeta de crédito?
Can I pay with traveler's checks?
¿Puedo pagar con cheques de viajero?
May I have a receipt?
¿Me puede dar el recibo?
Could you please . . . ?
¿Podría usted . . . , por favor?
Is the tip included?
¿Está incluida la propina?
Could you give me . . . ?
¿Podría darme . . . ?
Can you deliver it to my hotel?
¿Puede enviarlo a mi hotel?

Maybe you like to pack light and get your clothes laundered or dry cleaned when you're away. Or maybe you'll be away longer than just a few weeks. Here are

the words and phrases you'll need if you plan to visit
the local dry cleaner or laundromat:

Can you please dry clean this for me?
¿Puede usted limpiar esto en seco, por favor?
Can you press this for me, please?
¿Puede usted plancharme esto, por favor?
Can you repair this for me, please?
¿Puede usted remendarme esto, por favor?
There is a stain here.
Hay una mancha aquí.
Is this machine taken?
¿Está ocupada esta máquina?
This machine is broken.
Esta máquina no funciona.
Where can I buy detergent?
¿Dónde puedo comprar detergente?

▶ At the Dry Cleaner's

dry cleaner's	la tintorería
a hole	un hueco
a tear	un rasgón
a missing button	un botón perdido
a broken zipper	una cremallera rota
a stain	una mancha
I need it . . .	Lo/la necesito . . .
I need them . . .	Los/las necesito . . .

▶ At the Dry Cleaner's *(continued)*

today	hoy
tomorrow	mañana
in an hour	en una hora
this afternoon	esta tarde
tonight	esta noche
tomorrow morning	mañana por la mañana

▶ At the Laundromat

bleach	lejía
clothing	ropa
clothes dryer	secadora
detergent	detergente
laundromat	lavandería
washing machine	lavadora

▶ At the Hair Salon/Barber Shop

just a trim	solo un recorte
Please shave my . . .	Por favor, aféiteme . . .
beard	la barba
mustache	el bigote
sideburns	las patillas
barbershop	la barbería
beauty salon	el salón de belleza
blow dry	secar el pelo
bangs	el flequillo
to comb	peinar
curly	rizado

▶ At the Hair Salon/Barber Shop *(continued)*

hair	el pelo
a haircut	un corte de pelo
hairstyle	peinado
highlights	reflejos
long	largo
short	corto
a manicure	una manicura
a pedicure	una pedicura
a perm	una permanente
to shave	afeitarse
wavy	ondulado
a waxing	una depilación

▶ At the Shoe Repair Shop

arch	el empeine
boot	la bota
broken	roto/a
heel	el tacón
scuff	la raya
shoe	el zapato
shoelace	el cordón de zapato
sole	la suela

I need a shoe shine.
Necesito una limpieza de zapatos.
Can you repair this . . . for me?
¿Puede usted remendarme este/a . . . ?

▶ At the Camera Shop

battery	la pila
camera	la cámara
camera film	la película
exposures	las exposiciones
video camera	la cámara de video

Can you repair this camera?
¿Puede usted reparar esta cámara?
Do you have film for this camera?
¿Tiene usted película para esta cámara?
I'd like to have this film developed.
Quisiera que me revele este rollo.

Eating Out

In Chapter 2, you learned the words for many foods and food-related terms. Now here are some helpful phrases, with pronunciation, to help you out when you're making reservations, ordering your meal, or making special requests at a restaurant.

Do I need a reservation?
¿Necesito una reservación?
May I see a menu?
¿Puedo ver la carta?
How is this prepared?
¿Cómo se prepara esto?
What do you recommend?
¿Qúe recomienda usted?

What is this?
¿Qúe es esto?
What are today's specials?
¿Cuáles son los platos del día de hoy?
I'd like to try a regional dish.
Quisiera probar un plato típico de la región.
Can you please bring the check?
¿Me puede traer la cuenta, por favor?
Can I pay with a credit card?
¿Puedo pagar con tarjeta de crédito?
I'm a vegetarian.
Soy vegetariano/a.
I'm on a diet.
Estoy a régimen.
I can't have (eat/drink) . . .
No puedo comer/tomar . . .
I'm allergic to . . .
Soy alérgico/a a . . .

Looking for a Job

Traveling is good for your language skills, but an even better way to start speaking like the locals is to get a job in a Spanish-speaking country. If you're in school and have the opportunity to spend a semester abroad, you can find an internship that will help you improve your professional skills and your foreign language. And if you're out in the real world, there are many programs available to those interested in spending some time abroad. You can do volunteer

work, teach English, or maybe even get a job in your
career field.

▶ Looking for a Job

job	empleo
resume	curriculum profesional
cover letter	carta de acompañamiento
ability, skill	habilidad
help-wanted ad	anuncio de trabajo
interview	entrevista
salary, wages	salario
boss	jefe

Putting Together a Resume

If you're serious about your job search, it'll help
to have a good resume. If you've already got one in
English, you'll have to change a few things, but the
idea is the same. In your resume, include your name
and address, date of birth, education, work experi-
ence, and skills.

SAMPLE RESUME

Datos personales
Nombre y apellido: Janet Morton
Lugar y fecha de nacimiento: San Francisco, 5 de abril de 1979
Dirección: 3 calle Main, #15, Boston, MA 01905
Teléfono: 617-555-1234

Formación
El Colegio San Bernardo, 1993-1997, calificación de notable.
Licenciado en Educación Bilingüe, UCLA, 1997-2001.
Idiomas
Castellano: leído, hablado, escrito y traducido (nivel alto).
Italiano: leído y hablado (nivel medio).
Informática
Microsoft Office, HTML
Experiencia profesional
Profesora del programa Inglés Como Segundo Idioma, escuela de
   Boston. Septiembre de 2001-mayo de 2003.
Directora del programa Inglés Como Segundo Idioma, escuela de
   Boston. Junio de 2003-el día presente.

As you can see, the first section should cover *datos personales* (personal information). In the United States, it is inappropriate for the employer to ask about your age, let alone expect you to list it on your resume. In Spain and in some parts of Latin America, however, indicating the *fecha de nacimiento* (date of birth)—as well as *lugar de nacimiento* (place of birth)—is still appropriate.

The next section is *formación* or education. List all education, from your high school (*el colegio*) to your degrees. Next are *idiomas* (languages) and *informática* (computer skills). The last part of your resume should be a list of work experiences, starting with the earliest. In a more detailed resume, you can also include a description of each job.

Surfing the Web

Even if going abroad is not an option—or at least not an option as of yet, don't despair. You've got the whole world at your fingertips. All you need is your computer and a way to log on to the World Wide Web; you can visit faraway places where people speak Spanish and join in their conversations. Here's some vocabulary to help get you started.

▶ The Web

. (dot)	punto
/ (slash)	barra
tool	herramienta
The Net	Red
password	contraseña
e-mail	correo electrónico
printer	impresora
online	en línea
offline	fuera de línea
key	botón
Web page	página de la Web
home page	página principal
search	buscar
site	sitio

English to Spanish Dictionary

A

a little	poco
a lot	mucho
a while	un rato
ability	la habilidad
abroad	el extranjero
academic	escolástico
to achieve	conseguir
accomplice	el consorte
according to	según
across from	enfrente a, frente a
to act	actuar
actress	la actriz
actually	la verdad es que
address	la dirección
to address with tú	tutearse
adjective	el adjetivo
adverb	el adverbio
to advise	aconsejar

after	después de
afternoon	la tarde
again	otra vez
against	contra
Algeria	Argelia
Algerian	argelino
all	todo
almost	casi
alone	solo
already	ya
although	aunque
always	siempre
American	estadounidense
amusing	gracioso
ancient	antiguo
to announce	anunciar
to annoy	molestar, fastidiar
annoying	fastidioso
another	otro
answer	la respuesta, la solución
to answer	contestar, responder
antiperspirant	el antisudoral
apartment	el apartamento
to appear	aparecer
appetite	el apetito
appetizer	el antojito
applause	el aplauso

apple	la manzana
to approach	acercarse
April	abril
Argentinean	argentino
around	alrededor
around here	acá
to arrange	arreglar
to arrive	llegar
as much/many	cuanto
as soon as	en cuanto
to ask	pedir
to ask (a question)	preguntar
at least	lo menos
attempt	el intento
to attend	asistir
attention	la atención
attentive	atento
attitude	la actitud
to attribute	atribuir
August	agosto
aunt	la tía
Australian	australiano
Austrian	austríaco
author	el autor
authorization	la autorización
autobiography	la autobiografía
to award	otorgar

B

baby	el bebé
back cover	la contracubierta
backpack	la mochila
bad	mal(o)
bakery	la panadería
bank	el banco
banker	el bancario
to bathe	bañar
to be	ser
to be (located)	estar
to be able to	poder
to be bored	aburrirse
to be happy	alegrarse
to be quiet	callarse
to be surprised	sorprenderse
to be well behaved	comportarse bien
to be worth	valer
beach	la playa
beautiful	bello
because	porque
to become	hacerse
bed	la cama
bedroom	el dormitorio
before	antes
beforehand	antemano
to begin (to)	empezar (a), comenzar (a)
behind	detrás
Belgian	belga

Belgium	Bélgica
to believe	creer
to belong	pertenecer
bench	el banco
best	mejor
between	entre
bill	la cuenta
billion	los mil millones
birth	el nacimiento
birthday	el cumpleaños
black	negro
to blink	parpadear
blond	rubio
blue	azul
board	la pizarra
boat	el bote
body	el cuerpo
Bolivian	boliviano
book	el libro
bookstore	la librería
to bore	aburrir
bored, boring	aburrido
boss	el jefe, la jefa
both	ambos, ambas
to bother	molestar
to bother oneself	lastimarse
box	la caja
boy	el chico, el niño
boyfriend	el novio

Brazil	el Brasil
Brazilian	brasileño
bread	el pan
to break	romper(se)
to break (a bone)	quebrarse
to break (something)	quebrar
breakfast	el desayuno
bright	claro
to bring	traer
brother	el hermano
brotherhood	la hermandad
brown	café, marrón
to brush (teeth, hair)	cepillar(se)
building	el edificio
to burn	quemar
bus	el autobús
but	pero, mas
but (following a neg. statement)	sino
butter	la mantequilla
to buy	comprar

C

cab driver	el/la taxista
cake	la torta
to call	llamar
camp	el campamento
Canada	el Canadá

Canadian	canadiense
candy, sweet	el dulce
car	el coche
care	el cuidado
carrot	la zanahoria
case	el caso
cat	el gato
to catch a cold	constiparse
cauliflower	la coliflor
cautious	prevenido
certain	cierto
certainty	la certidumbre
chair	la silla
to change	cambiar
chapter	el capítulo
to chat	charlar
cheese	el queso
chef	el cocinero, la cocinera
chewing gum	el chicle
chicken	el pollo
child	el niño, la niña
Chilean	chileno
Chinese	chino
chocolate	el chocolate
to choke	ahogar, sofocar
chop (pork)	la chuleta
chore	la tarea
Christmas	la Navidad

church	la iglesia
city	la ciudad
class	la clase
clear	claro, transparente
clock	el reloj
to close	cerrar
close by	cerca
clothes	la ropa
cloudy	nublado
coffee	el café
coin	la moneda
cold	frío
college	la escuela universitaria, la universidad
Colombian	colombiano
to come	venir
to come in	entrar
to come to a halt	detenerse
comfortable	cómodo
common	común
community	la comunidad
company	la companía
to complain	quejarse
compromise	el arreglo
computer	la computadora
condom	el preservativo
to conjugate	conjugar
consort	el consorte
constipated (to be)	estar extreñido
contemplation	la contemplación

to continue	continuar, seguir
to contribute to	contribuir a
cook	el cocinero, la cocinera
to cook	cocinar
cookie	la galleta
corn	el maíz
correct	veraz
to cost	costar, valer
Costa Rican	costarricense
costume	el vestuario
to count	contar
country	el país
countryside	el campo
cousin	el primo, la prima
to cover	cubrir, tapar
cover letter	la carta de acompañamiento
to crash	chocar
cream	la crema
crime	el delito
to cross	atravesar, cruzar
Cuban	cubano
cup	la taza
current	actual
cute	guapo

D

damp	húmedo
to dance	bailar

dangerous	peligroso
Danish	danés
to dare to	atreverse
dark	oscuro
dark brown (eyes)	marrón
dark-haired	moreno
dash	el guión
date (day and month)	la fecha
date (appointment)	la cita
daughter	la hija
daughter-in-law	la nuera
day before yesterday	anteayer
day	el día
dear	estimado, querido
December	diciembre
to defend	defender
delight	el deleite
to demand	demandar
Denmark	Dinamarca
to deny	negarse a
to deserve	merecer
despite	a pesar de
despite (as)	con todo
to destroy	destruir
to die	morir
diet	la dieta
different	diferente
difficult	difícil

to dignify	dignificar
dining room	el comedor
dinner	la cena
to direct	dirigir
disagreement	la discordia
disappointment	la decepción
to discover	descubrir
to discuss	discutir
to disembark	desembarcar
to do	hacer
doctor	el médico, la médica
dog	el perro
doll	la muñeca
Dominican	dominicano
Dominican Republic	la República Dominicana
door	la puerta
downtown	el centro
dress	el vestido
to dress	vestir
dressed in	vestido de
dresser	el armario
drink	la bebida
to drink	beber, tomar
drinking glass	el vaso
to drive	conducir
duck	el pato
during	durante
Dutch	holandés

E

early	temprano
to earn	ganar
easy	fácil
to eat	comer
Ecuadorian	ecuatoriano
educated	culto
education	la enseñanza
egg	el huevo
eggplant	la berenjena
Egypt	Egipto
Egyptian	egipcio
eighteen	dieciocho
eighth	octavo
eighty	ochenta
either . . . or	o . . . o
eleven	once
e-mail	el correo electrónico
to end	concluir
end result	la culminación
energy	la energía
England	Inglaterra
English	inglés
to enter	entrar
environment	el medio ambiente
event	el suceso
everybody	todos
everything	todo

example	el ejemplo
except	excepto, salvo
exclamation mark	el signo de exclamación
excuse me	con permiso
exit	la salida
expansive	expansivo
to expect	imaginarse
expense	el gasto
to explain	explicar
eye	el ojo

F

face	la cara
facing	enfrente a, frente a
fact	el dato
fair	justo
to fall	caer
family	la familia
fan	el aficionado
fat	corpulento, gordo
father	el padre
father-in-law	el suegro
February	febrero
to feel	sentir
fever	la fiebre
few	pocos
fiancé	el novio

fiancée	la novia
field	el campo
fifth	quinto
fifty	cincuenta
to find one's place	colocarse
to find out	enterar(se)
fine (as in penalty)	la multa
to finish	acabar, terminar
first	primero
fish (for eating)	el pescado
fish	el pez
to fit	caber
five	cinco
floor	el piso
florist's shop	la florería
flower	la flor
fly	la mosca
to fly	volar
to follow	seguir
to force	obligar a
foreigner	el extranjero
fourth	cuarto
French	francés
fresh	fresco
Friday	el viernes
friend	el amigo
from	desde
fruit	la fruta
full of	lleno de

fun	divertido
funny	gracioso

G

garden	el jardín
to gather	recoger, reunirse
German	alemán
Germany	Alemania
to get	conseguir
to get a job	colocarse
to get angry	enfadarse, enojarse
to get annoyed	molestarse
to get burned	quemarse
to get dressed	vestirse
to get ready	arreglarse
to get together	reunirse
to get up	levantarse
to get used to	acostumbrarse
girl	la chica, la niña
girlfriend	la novia
to give	dar
to give as a gift	regalar
glove	el guante
to go	ir
to go out	salir
to go to bed	acostarse
to go to sleep	dormirse
God	Dios

gold	el oro
good	bueno
to govern	gobernar
to grab	coger, tomar
grandfather	el abuelo
grandmother	la abuela
grape	la uva
grapefruit	el pomelo
gray (color)	gris
gray (hair)	canoso
great	gran(de)
Greece	Grecia
Greek	griego
green	verde
greeting	el saludo
grocery store	el almacén
Guatemalan	guatemalteco
guest	el invitado
to guide	guiar
gym	el gimnasio

H

hair	el cabello, el pelo
Haitian	haitiano
half	medio
ham	el jamón
hand	la mano
handkerchief	el pañuelo

to happen	pasar
happiness	la alegría
happy	feliz
hat	el sombrero
to have	tener
to have fun	divertirse
to have lunch	almorzar
hazel	color de avellana
healthy	sano
to hear	oír
heat	el calor
heel	el tacón
height	la estatura
hello	hola
to help	ayudar
here	aquí
high	alto
history	la historia
home	la casa
Honduran	hondureño
to hope	esperar
hot	caliente
hour	la hora
house	la casa
how much/many?	cuánto
how?	cómo
hug	el abrazo
humid	húmedo
Hungarian	húngaro

Hungary	Hungría
hunger	la hambre
to hurry	apresurarse a
husband	el marido, el esposo

I

ice cream	el helado
if	si
in agreement	de acuerdo
in case	en caso de que
in front of	delante de
in order that	a fin de que
incredible	increíble
Indian	hindú
information	la información
inside	adentro, dentro de
to interest	interesar
interested	interesado
interesting	interesante
international	internacional
to invite to	invitar a
Iranian	iraní
Iraqi	iraquí
Ireland	Irlanda
Irish	irlandés
Israeli	israelí
Italian	italiano
itself	mismo

J

jacket	la chaqueta
January	enero
Japan	el Japón
Japanese	japonés
Jewish	judío
to join	reunir
Judaism	el judaísmo
juice	el jugo
July	julio
June	junio
just	justo, simple

K

button	el botón
key	la llave
kitchen	la cocina
to know	conocer, saber
Korea	Corea
Korean	coreano

L

language	el idioma
large	gran(de)
last name	el apellido
last	último
late	tarde

to laugh	reír
laundromat	la lavandería
lazy	holgazán
leaf	la hoja
to learn	aprender
to leave	quedar, salir
Lebanese	libanés
Lebanon	Líbano
lecture	la charla, la conferencia
left	izquierdo
leg	la pierna
legumes	las legumbres
less	menos
letter	la carta
library	la biblioteca
light	la luz
to light	encender
like that	así
like	como
to like	gustar(le)
to link	enlazar
to listen	escuchar
to live	vivir
long	largo
look	la mirada, el vistazo
to look for	buscar
to lose	perder
love	el amor
luck	la suerte

M

magazine	la revista
to make	hacer
man	el hombre
many	muchos
map	el mapa
March	marzo
market	el mercado
to marry (each other)	casar(se)
matter	el asunto, la cuestión
May	mayo
maybe	quizá, quizás, tal vez
to mean	significar
menu	la carta, el menú
Mexican	mexicano
microwave	el microondas
midday	mediodía
midnight	medianoche
milk	la leche
million	el millón
Miss	señorita, Srta.
mistake	el error
Monday	el lunes
money	el dinero, la plata
more	más
morning	la mañana
Moroccan	marroquí
Morocco	Marruecos
mother	la madre

motorcycle	la motocicleta
mountain	la montaña
mouth	la boca
to move	conmover
to move, change residence	mudar(se)
to move something closer	acercar
movie	la película
movies	el cine
Mr.	señor, Sr.
Mrs., Ms.	señora, Sra.
music	la música
must	deber
myself	mismo, misma

N

name	el nombre
nap	la siesta
nationality	la nacionalidad
near	cerca de
to need	necesitar
neither, either	tampoco
neither . . . nor	ni . . . ni
never	jamás, nunca
New York	Nueva York
New Yorker	neoyorquino
new	nuevo
news	las noticias
next	próximo

next to	al lado de
Nicaraguan	nicaragüense
nice	amable, lindo, simpático
night	la noche
no one	nadie
noise	el ruido
none	ninguno
Norway	Noruega
Norwegian	noruego
note	la nota
notebook	el cuaderno
nothing	nada
noun	el sustantivo
November	noviembre
nurse	la enfermera

O

October	octubre
office	la oficina
often	a menudo, muchas veces
old	viejo
on (top of)	sobre
on time	a tiempo
once	alguna vez
onion	la cebolla
only	sólo
open	abierto
to open	abrir

orange	la naranja
other	otro
ourselves	mismos, mismas
outside	fuera
over	encima
overcooked	recocido

P

page	la hoja, la página
Panama	el Panamá
Panamanian	panameño
pants	los pantalones
paper	el papel
Paraguayan	paraguayo
parents	los padres
Parisian	parisiense
park	el parque
party	la fiesta
pastry	el postre
pasture	el pasto
to pay	pagar
to pay attention	prestar atención
pear	la pera
pen	el bolígrafo, la pluma
performance (theater)	la representación
Peruvian	peruano
to pick up	levantar
piece	el pedazo

pillow	la almohada
pineapple	la piña
place	el lugar
plane	el avión
to play	jugar, tocar
please	por favor
Poland	Polonia
Polish	polaco
polite	educado
politics	la política
poor	pobre
Portuguese	portugués
possibly	posiblemente
to prefer	preferir
to prepare to	prepararse a
present (gift)	el regalo
present	el presente
president	el presidente, la presidenta
pretty	bonito, lindo
printer	la impresora
probably	probablemente
problem	el problema
public	público
Puerto Rican	puertorriqueño

Q

question	la cuestión
quiet	la quietud

R

to rain	llover
rain	la lluvia
rather	bastante, más bien
to read	leer
reader	el lector, la lectora
reading	la lectura
ready	listo
real	verdadero
really	efectivamente, verdaderamente
red	rojo
red (hair)	pelirrojo
religion	la religión
rest	descansar
(the) rest	los demás
restaurant	el restaurante
to return	regresar, volver
rich	rico
river	el río
road	el camino
room	el cuarto
Russian	ruso

S

salad	la ensalada
salt	la sal
Salvadoran	salvadoreño
same	mismo

Saturday	el sábado
sauce	la salsa
sausage	el chorizo, la salchicha
to say	decir
to say goodbye	despedirse
sea	el mar
seafront	el malecón
seafood	los mariscos
second	segundo
second to last	penúltimo
to see	ver
to sell	vender
to send	enviar, mandar
September	septiembre
seventh	séptimo
seventy	setenta
shirt	la camisa
shoe store	la zapatería
shop	la tienda
shower	la ducha
shrimp	el camarón, la gamba
sick	enfermo
side	el lado
to sit	sentarse
site	el sitio
sixth	sexto
to sleep	dormir
small	pequeño
to smell	oler

smile	la sonrisa
to smoke	fumar
so	así
soap	el jabón
socks	las medias
soon	pronto
soup	la sopa
Spain	España
Spanish (Castilian) language	castellano
Spanish (from Spain)	español
to speak	hablar
to stop	parar, detener
story	la historia
strange	raro
street	la calle
student	el/la estudiante
study	el estudio
to study	aprender, estudiar
subjunctive	subjuntivo
sugar	el azúcar
sun	el sol
Sunday	el domingo
to swim	nadar

T

table	la mesa
Taiwanese	taiwanés
to take	tomar

to take a bath	bañarse
take off	quitar(se)
tall	alto
to teach how to	enseñar a
telephone (number)	el teléfono
television	la televisión
tenth	décimo
Thai	tailandés
Thailand	Tailandia
to thank	agradecer
that one	aquél, ése
that	aquel, ese
that	que, quien
theater	el teatro
themselves	mismos, mismas
there	donde
thief	el ladrón, la ladrona
third	tercero
thirteen	trece
this one	éste
thought	el pensamiento
thousand	mil
Thursday	el jueves
ticket	el boleto
time	el tiempo, la vez
tired	cansado
to the side of	al lado de
today	hoy
together	juntos

tomorrow	mañana
too, also	también
town	el pueblo
traffic	el tráfico
train	el tren
to translate	traducir
translation	la traducción
trash	la basura
to travel	viajar
tree	el árbol
Tuesday	el martes
twin	el gemelo

U

umbrella	el paraguas
under	debajo
United Kingdom	Reino Unido
United States	los Estados Unidos
united	unido
university	la universidad
until	hasta
Uruguayan	uruguayo
useful	útil

V

vegetables (green)	los vegetales
vegetables	las legumbres

Venezuelan	venezolano
verb	el verbo
very	muy
Vietnamese	vietnamita

W

waiter	el camarero
waitress	la camarera
to walk	andar, caminar
wall	la pared
to want	querer
to wash	lavar(se)
water	el agua
way	el camino
weather	el tiempo
Wednesday	el miércoles
week	la semana
weekend	el fin de semana
welcome	bienvenidos
well	bien
what	qué
when	cuándo, cuando
where	dónde, donde
which	cuál, cual
while	mientras
white	blanco
who	quién, quien
whoever	quienquiera

why	por qué
will	la voluntad
wind	el viento
with me	conmigo
with you	contigo
without	sin (que)
woman	la mujer
to write	escribir

Y

year	el año
yes	sí
yesterday	ayer

Z

zero	cero

Spanish to English Dictionary

A

abierto	open
abril	April
abrir	to open
la abuela	grandmother
el abuelo	grandfather
aburrido	boring, bored
aburrir	to bore
aburrirse	to be bored
acá	around here
acabar	to finish
acercar	to move something closer
acostar	to put to bed
acostarse	to go to bed
acostumbrarse	to get used to
adentro	inside
el adjetivo	adjective
adónde	to where
agosto	August

agradecer	to thank
el agua	water
alemán	German
Alemania	Germany
algo	something
alguien	someone, somebody
algún	some
algunas veces	sometimes
alguna vez	once, sometime
al lado de	next to, to the side of
el almacén	grocery store
la almohada	pillow
almorzar	to have lunch
alrededor	around
amable	nice
ambos, ambas	both
a menos que	unless
el amigo	friend
el amor	love
andar	to walk
anteayer	day before yesterday
antiguo	former, ancient
el antisudoral	antiperspirant
el apartamento	apartment
el apellido	last name
apresurarse a	to hurry
el árbol	tree
Argelia	Algeria
argelino	Algerian

argentino	Argentinean
arreglarse	to get ready
el arreglo	compromise
asistir	to attend
el asunto	matter
a tiempo	on time
atravesar	to cross
australiano	Australian
austríaco	Austrian
el autobús	bus
a veces	sometimes
el avión	plane
ayer	yesterday
ayudar	to help

B

bañar	to bathe
bañarse	to take a bath
la basura	trash
beber	to drink
la bebida	drink
belga	Belgian
Bélgica	Belgium
bello	beautiful, lovely
la biblioteca	library
bien	well
bienvenidos	welcome
el boleto	ticket

el bolígrafo	pen
boliviano	Bolivian
bonito	pretty
el bote	boat
el botón	key
el Brasil	Brazil
brasileño	Brazilian
bueno	good
la bufanda	scarf
buscar	to look for
el buzón	mailbox

C

el cabello	hair
caber	to fit
cada	each
el café	coffee
la caja	box
caliente	hot
la calle	street
el calor	heat
la cama	bed
la camarera	waitress
el camarero	waiter
caminar	to walk
el camino	road, way
el camión	truck
la camiseta	shirt

el campamento	camp
el campanario	bell tower
el campo	field, countryside
el Canadá	Canada
canadiense	Canadian
cansado	tired
la carta	menu, letter
la casa	house, home
castellano	Spanish language
el catedrático	professor
el catolicismo	Catholicism
católico	Catholic
la cena	dinner
el centro	downtown
cepillar(se)	to brush (teeth, hair)
cerca (de)	close by, near
cero	zero
cerrar	to close
la cesta	wastebasket
la chaqueta	jacket
la charla	lecture
chileno	Chilean
los chiles rellenos	stuffed peppers
chino	Chinese
el cine	movies
la cita	date
la ciudad	city
el coche	car
la cocina	kitchen

cocinar	to cook
el cocinero, la cocinera	cook, chef
la cocineta	kitchenette
colombiano	Colombian
color de avellana	hazel
comer	to eat
cómo	how?
como	as, like
cómodo	comfortable
la companía	company
comprar	to buy
la comunidad	community
con	with
concluir	to end, to conclude
conducir	to drive
con permiso	excuse me
constiparse	to catch a cold
con tal de que	provided that
contar	to tell, to count
contigo	with you
continuar	to continue
con todo	despite, as
Corea	Korea
coreano	Korean
el correo electrónico	e-mail
correr	to run
costar	to cost
costarricense	Costa Rican
cruzar	to cross

el cuaderno	notebook
cuál	which?
cual	which
cualquier	whichever
cuándo	when?
cuando	when, then
cuánto	how much/many?
cuanto	as much/many
cuarto	fourth
el cuarto	room, bedroom
cubano	Cuban
la cuenta	bill

D

danés	Danish
dar	to give
darse cuenta	to realize
el dato	fact, piece of information
de acogida	foster
de acuerdo	in agreement
debajo	under
deber	must
la decepción	disappointment
decir	to say
delante de	in front of
de manera que	so that
demasiado	too (adverb modifying an adjective)
demás	the rest

dentro de	inside
descubrir	to discover
desde	from, since
deseable	desirable
despedirse	to say goodbye
después de	after
detrás	behind
el día	day
diciembre	December
Dinamarca	Denmark
el dinero	money
la dirección	address
dirigir	to direct
divertido	fun
divertirse	to have fun
el domingo	Sunday
dominicano	Dominican
dónde	where?
donde	where, there
dormir	to sleep
dormirse	to go to sleep
la ducha	shower
el dulce	candy, sweet
durante	during

E

echarse a	to start to
ecuatoriano	Ecuadorian

el edificio	building
emocionante	thrilling, moving
empezar (a)	to begin (to)
encima	over
en cuanto	as soon as
enero	January
enfermo	sick
enfrente a	facing, across from
entrar	to come in, to enter
entre	between
escribir	to write
la escritura	writing
escuchar	to listen
ése	that one
ese	that
España	Spain
español	Spanish (from Spain)
los Estados Unidos	United States
estadounidense	American
estar	to be (located)
éste	this one
este	this
el extranjero	foreigner, abroad
extraño	strange

F

fácil	easy
la familia	family

febrero	February
la fecha	date
la fiesta	party
el fin de semana	weekend
finlandés	Finnish
francés	French
frente a	facing, across from
frío	cold
fuera	outside
fumar	to smoke
el fútbol	soccer

G

el gasto	expense
la gente	people
el/la gerente	manager
gobernar	to govern
gran(de)	large, great
Grecia	Greece
griego	Greek
guatemalteco	Guatemalan
gustar(le)	to like, to be pleasing to

H

hablar	to speak
hacer	to make, to do
haitiano	Haitian

la hambre	hunger
harto de	sick of
hasta	until
hindú	Indian
la historia	history, story
la hoja	leaf, page
hola	hello
holandés	Dutch
hondureño	Honduran
la hora	hour
el horario	schedule
hoy	today
húngaro	Hungarian
Hungría	Hungary

I

el idioma	language
la iglesia	church
increíble	incredible
la información	information
Inglaterra	England
inglés	English
interesante	interesting
internacional	international, among nations
el invitado	guest
invitar a	to invite to
ir	to go
iraní	Iranian

iraquí	Iraqi
Irlanda	Ireland
irlandés	Irish
israelí	Israeli
italiano	Italian
izquierdo	left

J

el jabón	soap
jamás	never
el Japón	Japan
japonés	Japanese
el jardín	garden
judío	Jewish
el jueves	Thursday
julio	July
junio	June
juntos	together

L

el lado	side
la langosta	lobster
la lavandería	Laundromat
lavar(se)	to wash
leer	to read
levantarse	to wake up, to get up
libanés	Lebanese

Líbano	Lebanon
la librería	bookstore
el libro	book
la llave	key
llegar	to arrive
llover	to rain
el lugar	place
el lunes	Monday

M

madrileño	from Madrid
mal(o)	bad
mandar	to send
la mañana	morning
mañana	tomorrow
el mapa	map
maquillarse	to put on makeup
marroquí	Moroccan
Marruecos	Morocco
el martes	Tuesday
marzo	March
más	more
mas	but
más bien	rather
mayo	May
mayor	older
las medias	socks
el médico, la médica	doctor

mediodía	midday
medir	to measure
el mercado	market
mexicano	Mexican
el miércoles	Wednesday
mil	thousand
el millón	million
el millonario	millionaire
los mil millones	billion
la mochila	backpack
la montaña	mountain
el mundo	world
muy	very

N

la nacionalidad	nationality
nada	nothing
nadar	to swim
nadie	no one
necesitar	to need
negarse a	to deny, to refuse
neocelandés	New Zealander
neoyorquino	New Yorker
nevar	to snow
nicaragüense	Nicaraguan
ninguno	none
ni . . . ni	neither . . . nor

la noche	night
el nombre	name
norteamericano	American
Noruega	Norway
noruego	Norwegian
noviembre	November
Nueva York	New York
Nueva Zelanda	New Zealand
nuevo	new
nunca	never

O

octavo	eighth
octubre	October
o . . . o	either . . . or
la opinión	opinion
otra vez	again
otro	other, another

P

pagar	to pay
el país	country
el Panamá	Panama
panameño	Panamanian
los pantalones	pants
el pañuelo	handkerchief

paraguayo	Paraguayan
para que	so that
parar	to stop
parisiense	Parisian
el parque	park
la película	movie
perder	to lose
el perdón	forgiveness
pero	but
peruano	Peruvian
la pizarra	board
la playa	beach
poco	a little
polaco	Polish
Polonia	Poland
poner	to put
ponerse a	to start to
por	by
por favor	please
por qué	why
porque	because
preferir	to prefer
el preservativo	condom
el/la presidente	president
primero	first
público	public
el pueblo	town
la puerta	door
puertorriqueño	Puerto Rican

Q

qué	what?
que	what, that
querer	to want
querido	dear
quién	who?
quien	who, that
quienquiera	whoever
quinto	fifth
quizá, quizás	maybe

R

regresar	to return
Reino Unido	United Kingdom
la religión	religion
la República Dominicana	Dominican Republic
el restaurante	restaurant
el río	river
romance	Romance (language)
la ropa	clothes
ruso	Russian

S

el sábado	Saturday
saber	to know
la salida	exit
salir	to go out, to leave

el saludo	greeting
salvadoreño	Salvadoran
segundo	second
la semana	week
señor, Sr.	Mr.
señora, Sra.	Mrs., Ms.
señorita, Srta.	Miss
septiembre	September
séptimo	seventh
ser	to be
sexto	sixth
sí	yes
si	if
siempre	always
sin que	without
el sitio	site
sobre	on, on top of
sólo	only
solo	alone
sudanés	Sudanese
la Suiza	Switzerland
suizo	Swiss
la superficie	surface
el sustantivo	noun

T

tailandés	Thai
Tailandia	Thailand

taiwanés	Taiwanese
tan . . . como	as . . . as
tanto	so much
tarde	late
la tarde	afternoon
el/la taxista	cab driver
la taza	cup
el teatro	theater
temprano	early
tener	to have
el tiempo	time, weather
la tienda	shop
la traducción	translation
traducir	to translate
tutearse	to address with tú

U

último	last
único	only, unique
unívoco	one to one
uno	one
uruguayo	Uruguayan
útil	useful

V

valer	to be worth, to cost
venezolano	Venezuelan

venir	to come
ver	to see
el verano	summer
la vez	time (occasion)
viajar	to travel
el viernes	Friday
vietnamita	Vietnamese
volver	to return
vos	you, informal/singular \ (in parts of Río de la Plata region)

Y

ya	already, now

Z

la zapatilla de deportes	sneaker
el zapato	shoe

Verb Tables

hablar (to speak)/Regular –AR verb

	present	subjunctive
yo	hablo	hable
tú	hablas	hables
él	habla	hable
nosotros	hablamos	hablemos
vosotros	habláis	habléis
ellos	hablan	hablen
	preterite	imperfect
yo	hablé	hablaba
tú	hablaste	hablabas
él	habló	hablaba
nosotros	hablamos	hablábamos
vosotros	hablasteis	hablabais
ellos	hablaron	hablaban
	future	conditional
yo	hablaré	hablaría
tú	hablarás	hablarías
él	hablará	hablaría
nosotros	hablaremos	hablaríamos
vosotros	hablaréis	hablaríais
ellos	hablarán	hablarían
imperfect subjunctive	form 1	form 2
yo	hablara	hablase
tú	hablaras	hablases
él	hablara	hablase
nosotros	habláramos	hablásemos
vosotros	hablarais	hablaseis
ellos	hablaran	hablasen
	command	present participle
(tú)	habla	hablando
	no hables	
(Ud.)	hable	
(nosotros)	hablemos	past participle
(vosotros)	hablad	hablado
	no habléis	
(Uds.)	hablen	

vender (to sell) / Regular −ER verb

	present	subjunctive
yo	vendo	venda
tú	vendes	vendas
él	vende	venda
nosotros	vendemos	vendamos
vosotros	vendéis	vendáis
ellos	venden	vendan
	preterite	imperfect
yo	vendí	vendía
tú	vendiste	vendías
él	vendió	vendía
nosotros	vendimos	vendíamos
vosotros	vendisteis	vendíais
ellos	vendieron	vendían
	future	conditional
yo	venderé	vendería
tú	venderás	venderías
él	venderá	vendería
nosotros	venderemos	venderíamos
vosotros	venderéis	venderíais
ellos	venderán	venderían
imperfect subjunctive	form 1	form 2
yo	vendiera	vendiese
tú	vendieras	vendieses
él	vendiera	vendiese
nosotros	vendiéramos	vendiésemos
vosotros	vendierais	vendieseis
ellos	vendieran	vendiesen
	command	present participle
(tú)	vende	vendiendo
	no vendas	
(Ud.)	venda	
(nosotros)	vendamos	past participle
(vosotros)	vended	vendido
	no vendáis	
(Uds.)	vendan	

vivir (to live) / Regular –IR verb

	present	subjunctive
yo	vivo	viva
tú	vives	vivas
él	vive	viva
nosotros	vivimos	vivamos
vosotros	vivís	viváis
ellos	viven	vivan
	preterite	imperfect
yo	viví	vivía
tú	viviste	vivías
él	vivió	vivía
nosotros	vivimos	vivíamos
vosotros	vivisteis	vivíais
ellos	vivieron	vivían
	future	conditional
yo	viviré	viviría
tú	vivirás	vivirías
él	vivirá	viviría
nosotros	viviremos	viviríamos
vosotros	viviréis	viviríais
ellos	vivirán	vivirían
imperfect subjunctive	form 1	form 2
yo	viviera	viviese
tú	vivieras	vivieses
él	viviera	viviese
nosotros	viviéramos	viviésemos
vosotros	vivierais	vivieseis
ellos	vivieran	viviesen
	command	present participle
(tú)	vive	viviendo
	no vivas	
(Ud.)	viva	
(nosotros)	vivamos	past participle
(vosotros)	vivid	vivido
	no viváis	
(Uds.)	vivan	

cerrar (to close) / Stem-changing (E > IE) –AR verb

	present	subjunctive
yo	cierro	cierre
tú	cierras	cierres
él	cierra	cierre
nosotros	cerramos	cerremos
vosotros	cerráis	cerréis
ellos	cierran	cierren
	preterite	imperfect
yo	cerré	cerraba
tú	cerraste	cerrabas
él	cerró	cerraba
nosotros	cerramos	cerrábamos
vosotros	cerrasteis	cerrabais
ellos	cerraron	cerraban
	future	conditional
yo	cerraré	cerraría
tú	cerrarás	cerrarías
él	cerrará	cerraría
nosotros	cerraremos	cerraríamos
vosotros	cerraréis	cerraríais
ellos	cerrarán	cerrarían
imperfect subjunctive	form 1	form 2
yo	cerrara	cerrase
tú	cerraras	cerrases
él	cerrara	cerrase
nosotros	cerráramos	cerrásemos
vosotros	cerrarais	cerraseis
ellos	cerraran	cerrasen
	command	present participle
(tú)	cierra	cerrando
	no cierres	
(Ud.)	cierre	
(nosotros)	cerremos	past participle
(vosotros)	cerrad	cerrado
	no cerréis	
(Uds.)	cierren	

conocer (to know) / Spelling-change (C > ZC) –ER verb

	present	*subjunctive*
yo	conozco	conozca
tú	conoces	conozcas
él	conoce	conozca
nosotros	conocemos	conozcamos
vosotros	conocéis	conozcáis
ellos	conocen	conozcan
	preterite	*imperfect*
yo	conocí	conocía
tú	conociste	conocías
él	conoció	conocía
nosotros	conocimos	conocíamos
vosotros	conocisteis	conocíais
ellos	conocieron	conocían
	future	*conditional*
yo	conoceré	conocería
tú	conocerás	conocerías
él	conocerá	conocería
nosotros	conoceremos	conoceríamos
vosotros	conoceréis	conoceríais
ellos	conocerán	conocerían
imperfect subjunctive	*form 1*	*form 2*
yo	conociera	conociese
tú	conocieras	conocieses
él	conociera	conociese
nosotros	conociéramos	conociésemos
vosotros	conocierais	conocieseis
ellos	conocieran	conociesen
	command	*present participle*
(tú)	conoce	conociendo
	no conozcas	
(Ud.)	conozca	
(nosotros)	conozcamos	*past participle*
(vosotros)	conoced	conocido
	no conozcáis	
(Uds.)	conozcan	

dar (to give) / Irregular –AR verb

	present	subjunctive
yo	doy	dé
tú	das	des
él	da	dé
nosotros	damos	demos
vosotros	dais	deis
ellos	dan	den
	preterite	imperfect
yo	di	daba
tú	diste	dabas
él	dio	daba
nosotros	dimos	dábamos
vosotros	disteis	dabais
ellos	dieron	daban
	future	conditional
yo	daré	daría
tú	darás	darías
él	dará	daría
nosotros	daremos	daríamos
vosotros	daréis	daríais
ellos	darán	darían
imperfect subjunctive	form 1	form 2
yo	diera	diese
tú	dieras	dieses
él	diera	diese
nosotros	diéramos	diésemos
vosotros	dicrais	dieseis
ellos	dieran	diesen
	command	present participle
(tú)	da	dando
	no des	
(Ud.)	dé	
(nosotros)	demos	past participle
(vosotros)	dad	dado
	no deis	
(Uds.)	den	

dormir (to sleep) / Stem-changing (O > UE) –IR verb

	present	subjunctive
yo	duermo	duerma
tú	duermes	duermas
él	duerme	duerma
nosotros	dormimos	durmamos
vosotros	dormís	durmáis
ellos	duermen	duerman
	preterite	imperfect
yo	dormí	dormía
tú	dormiste	dormías
él	durmió	dormía
nosotros	dormimos	dormíamos
vosotros	dormisteis	dormíais
ellos	durmieron	dormían
	future	conditional
yo	dormiré	dormiría
tú	dormirás	dormirías
él	dormirá	dormiría
nosotros	dormiremos	dormiríamos
vosotros	dormiréis	dormiríais
ellos	dormirán	dormirían
imperfect subjunctive	form 1	form 2
yo	durmiera	durmiese
tú	durmieras	durmieses
él	durmiera	durmiese
nosotros	durmiéramos	durmiésemos
vosotros	durmierais	durmieseis
ellos	durmieran	durmiesen
	command	present participle
(tú)	duerme	durmiendo
	no duermas	
(Ud.)	duerma	
(nosotros)	durmamos	past participle
(vosotros)	dormid	dormido
	no durmáis	
(Uds.)	duerman	

estar (to be) / Irregular –AR verb

	present	subjunctive
yo	estoy	esté
tú	estás	estés
él	está	esté
nosotros	estamos	estemos
vosotros	estáis	estéis
ellos	están	estén
	preterite	*imperfect*
yo	estuve	estaba
tú	estuviste	estabas
él	estuvo	estaba
nosotros	estuvimos	estábamos
vosotros	estuvisteis	estabais
ellos	estuvieron	estaban
	future	*conditional*
yo	estaré	estaría
tú	estarás	estarías
él	estará	estaría
nosotros	estaremos	estaríamos
vosotros	estaréis	estaríais
ellos	estarán	estarían
imperfect subjunctive	*form 1*	*form 2*
yo	estuviera	estuviese
tú	estuvieras	estuvieses
él	estuviera	estuviese
nosotros	estuviéramos	estuviésemos
vosotros	estuvierais	estuvieseis
ellos	estuvieran	estuviesen
	command	*present participle*
(tú)	está	estando
	no estés	
(Ud.)	esté	
(nosotros)	estemos	*past participle*
(vosotros)	estad	estado
	no estéis	
(Uds.)	estén	

hacer (to do, to make) / Irregular –ER verb

	present	subjunctive
yo	hago	haga
tú	haces	hagas
él	hace	haga
nosotros	hacemos	hagamos
vosotros	hacéis	hagáis
ellos	hacen	hagan
	preterite	imperfect
yo	hice	hacía
tú	hiciste	hacías
él	hizo	hacía
nosotros	hicimos	hacíamos
vosotros	hicisteis	hacíais
ellos	hicieron	hacían
	future	conditional
yo	haré	haría
tú	harás	harías
él	hará	haría
nosotros	haremos	haríamos
vosotros	haréis	haríais
ellos	harán	harían
imperfect subjunctive	form 1	form 2
yo	hiciera	hiciese
tú	hicieras	hicieses
él	hiciera	hiciese
nosotros	hiciéramos	hiciésemos
vosotros	hicierais	hicieseis
ellos	hicieran	hiciesen
	command	present participle
(tú)	haz	haciendo
	no hagas	
(Ud.)	haga	
(nosotros)	hagamos	past participle
(vosotros)	haced	hecho
	no hagáis	
(Uds.)	hagan	

ir (to go) / Irregular –IR verb

	present	*subjunctive*
yo	voy	vaya
tú	vas	vayas
él	va	vaya
nosotros	vamos	vayamos
vosotros	vais	vayáis
ellos	van	vayan
	preterite	*imperfect*
yo	fui	iba
tú	fuiste	ibas
él	fue	iba
nosotros	fuimos	íbamos
vosotros	fuisteis	ibais
ellos	fueron	iban
	future	*conditional*
yo	iré	iría
tú	irás	irías
él	irá	iría
nosotros	iremos	iríamos
vosotros	iréis	iríais
ellos	irán	irían
imperfect subjunctive	*form 1*	*form 2*
yo	fuera	fuese
tú	fueras	fueses
él	fuera	fuese
nosotros	fuéramos	fuésemos
vosotros	fuerais	fueseis
ellos	fueran	fuesen
	command	*present participle*
(tú)	ve	yendo
	no vayas	
(Ud.)	vaya	
(nosotros)	vamos	*past participle*
	no vayamos	ido
(vosotros)	id	
	no vayáis	
(Uds.)	vayan	

saber (to know) / Irregular –ER verb

	present	subjunctive
yo	sé	sepa
tú	sabes	sepas
él	sabe	sepa
nosotros	sabemos	sepamos
vosotros	sabéis	sepáis
ellos	saben	sepan
	preterite	imperfect
yo	supe	sabía
tú	supiste	sabías
él	supo	sabía
nosotros	supimos	sabíamos
vosotros	supisteis	sabíais
ellos	supieron	sabían
	future	conditional
yo	sabré	sabría
tú	sabrás	sabrías
él	sabrá	sabría
nosotros	sabremos	sabríamos
vosotros	sabréis	sabríais
ellos	sabrán	sabrían
imperfect subjunctive	form 1	form 2
yo	supiera	supiese
tú	supieras	supieses
él	supiera	supiese
nosotros	supiéramos	supiésemos
vosotros	supierais	supieseis
ellos	supieran	supiesen
	command	present participle
(tú)	sabe	sabiendo
	no sepas	
(Ud.)	sepa	
(nosotros)	sepamos	past participle
(vosotros)	sabed	sabido
	no sepáis	
(Uds.)	sepan	

ser (to be) / Irregular –ER verb

	present	subjunctive
yo	soy	sea
tú	eres	seas
él	es	sea
nosotros	somos	seamos
vosotros	sois	seáis
ellos	son	sean
	preterite	imperfect
yo	fui	era
tú	fuiste	eras
él	fue	era
nosotros	fuimos	éramos
vosotros	fuisteis	erais
ellos	fueron	eran
	future	conditional
yo	seré	sería
tú	serás	serías
él	será	sería
nosotros	seremos	seríamos
vosotros	seréis	seríais
ellos	serán	serían
imperfect subjunctive	form 1	form 2
yo	fuera	fuese
tú	fueras	fueses
él	fuera	fuese
nosotros	fuéramos	fuésemos
vosotros	fuerais	fueseis
ellos	fueran	fuesen
	command	present participle
(tú)	sé	siendo
	no seas	
(Ud.)	sea	
(nosotros)	seamos	past participle
(vosotros)	sed	sido
	no seáis	
(Uds.)	sean	

tener (to have) / Irregular –ER verb

	present	subjunctive
yo	tengo	tenga
tú	tienes	tengas
él	tiene	tenga
nosotros	tenemos	tengamos
vosotros	tenéis	tengáis
ellos	tienen	tengan
	preterite	imperfect
yo	tuve	tenía
tú	tuviste	tenías
él	tuvo	tenía
nosotros	tuvimos	teníamos
vosotros	tuvisteis	teníais
ellos	tuvieron	tenían
	future	conditional
yo	tendré	tendría
tú	tendrás	tendrías
él	tendrá	tendría
nosotros	tendremos	tendríamos
vosotros	tendréis	tendríais
ellos	tendrán	tendrían
imperfect subjunctive	form 1	form 2
yo	tuviera	tuviese
tú	tuvieras	tuvieses
él	tuviera	tuviese
nosotros	tuviéramos	tuviésemos
vosotros	tuvierais	tuvieseis
ellos	tuvieran	tuviesen
	command	present participle
(tú)	ten	teniendo
	no tengas	
(Ud.)	tenga	
(nosotros)	tengamos	past participle
(vosotros)	tened	tenido
	no tengáis	
(Uds.)	tengan	

Index